THELMA: A CHILD OF GOD
by
THELMA HAYMAN

CHILD OR GOD

THELMA: A CHILD OF GOD

by

THELMA HAYMAN

© 1987 Bridge Publishing (UK)
Monmouth, Gwent, UK.

All rights reserved

No part of this publication may be reproduced or transmitted in any form or by any means, electronic or mechanical, including photocopy, recording, or any information and retrieval system, without the written permission of the publisher.

ISBN 1/85030/005/4

Phototypeset by Input Typesetting Ltd., London SW19 8DR
Printed by Anchor Brendon, Tiptree, Essex

Contents

Foreword

It is my privilege to commend this book, written as it is from the heart by Mrs. Thelma Hayman. Anyone who knows Thelma will immediately testify to her Christian commitment and her high resolve to share her faith with any who care to listen. Her life could not be described as easy, far from it – orphaned in early childhood, she was dogged by ill-health and still is, to a large extent.

Thelma spent many years in and out of hospital for treatment, and that she is still alive can only be due to the goodness and faithfulness of God. She has written here of her experiences in simple and straightforward terms with no attempt to embellish the facts, and with no attempt at self-glorification.

In the telling of her life experiences, Thelma has but two aims – to glorify the Lord she loves and serves, and to introduce readers to Him that they too might come to know Him as the One who can bring eternal life and the forgiveness of sins. Her early years were spent in the care of the Muller Homes and she acknowledges that it was due to the love and care that she received there that led her to a living faith in our Lord Jesus Christ.

Ponder as you read, and ask whether you personally have that same faith in God through Christ. I detect another reason why this testimony has been written, perhaps not detected by Thelma herself, and that is that the faith of believers might be strengthened as they think on the goodness of God to her.

J. Cowan
Muller House

Acknowledgements

Acknowledgements and thanks are due and are very gratefully tendered for the kind way in which friends have composed poems and hymns for me; many of whom are personal friends of ours. Many of the hymns used are those that permission has been given and ones that we as orphans learnt off by heart from our own Ashley Down Orphans' Hymn Book, *especially put together for 'Mullers Orphanage' in 1908*. A. T. Bannister, Ron Bridle, G. Lane, I. Y. Ewan, E. G. Lessey, W. R. Holt, L. H. Edmunds, E. E. Hewitt, J. Wallace 1839. Emily Miller 1867, Frances Havergal 1838, A. Holness, (W. Cooper, 1 verse used), A. Toplady 1 verse used. (F. Alexander 1848 1 verse used) Ann Gilbert 1782, Fanny Crosby. (Bernard of Clairvaux 1 verse used), S. Stennett, E. H. Jenkins 1 verse used.

Thanks go especially to my brother Herbert and sister Flora for the help given from the family's personal correspondence. Every effort has been made to trace the owners of copyright, but if any rights have been unwittingly infringed, sincere apologies are tendered, and the kind permission is here requested that would have been asked in private correspondence.

All Scripture quotations are from the KJV.

CHAPTER ONE

Early Days

Day after day two young children played in the sun. On the horizon dark clouds were forming. The children continued to play, innocently unaware of the terrible storm that was about to break and change their lives for ever.

It was a great treat each time the family went to visit Grandmother and Grandfather in Saltash. The grandparents had a farm, with shire-horses and other animals. The sheepdogs were a great attraction, with the country life which the whole family just loved. Like all happy families time used to pass by so quickly, and the fresh air each day would enable the family to sleep well at night. This was a glorious part of the County of Devon. How they enjoyed God's wonderful creation, and would talk and sing of His great goodness to mankind as a whole, as well as to them as a family.

By the time Herbert the oldest child was six, and Mary-Flora was five, Mother and Father welcomed another baby girl into their home. Yes, this was me. There was great joy at the thought of another baby girl born into our family. The Minister of Wembury called on our mother and father and the little family who had now moved to a larger country cottage.

The Minister was welcomed into the home and it was not long before they were drinking a cup of tea together and the Minister was helping them choose a name for me. The Minister said, "Why not call her Thelma, which means 'The Will of God'." It proved to be a good choice of name and later on we will see why!

The picturesque church was not far away and there was such a peace as one climbed the steep hillside to Wembury Church. On a summer Sunday afternoon or evening, and sometimes in the morning when the parents of the village

1

of Wembury went to collect their children from Sunday School, they would hear the children singing their hymns and their little worshipping hearts would be heard to sing,

I Love to Hear the Story

I love to hear the story
Which Angel voices tell,
How once the King of Glory,
Came down on earth to dwell;
I am both weak and sinful,
But this I surely know,
The Lord came down to save me,
Because He loved me so.

I'm glad my blessed Saviour
Was once a child like me,
To show how pure and holy
His little ones might be;
O may I try to follow
His footsteps here below,
Who never will forget me,
Because He loved me so!

To sing His love and mercy
My sweetest songs I'll raise,
And though I cannot see Him
I know He hears my praise!
For He has kindly promised
That I shall surely go
To sing among His angels
Because He loved me so.

Once the theme was on the text, "God is Faithful", also "My God shall supply all your needs according to His riches in glory by Christ Jesus." Phil. 4 v 19. Many answers of prayer in this book will be told of the faithfulness of our loving Heavenly Father.

Here is one such answer of the faithfulness of God at a time when the Counties of Devon and Cornwall were suffering from a long drought. Some praying farmers, fearing to lose their crops for want of water, asked their Minister to convene a special prayer meeting to ask God for the rain they so greatly needed. The Minister arrived early to greet the friends as they came. Amongst them was little Mary-Flora and Herbert-William from the Sunday School. Mary-Flora carried the big family umbrella. It was so large as to be a burden for one so little to carry as she was only five, so Herbert her brother helped her to carry it as he was six!

The Minister of Wembury Church, quite astonished, looked at the children and said, "What can you mean by bringing the large family umbrella for it's such a lovely day?"

The children, so trusting, looked up in surprise and said, "Please we thought, sir, as we were going to talk to Jesus in prayer and ask in His Name that our loving Heavenly Father would send us rain, we must bring Mother and Father's umbrella, for we will need it when God sends us our rain for Gran and Grandad's farm, and all the other places in Devon and Cornwall. You see, sir, as Dad is very sick, Mother is caring for him, she is looking after our Aunts also and they have such awful coughs, so bad that Doctor is calling two times a week. We do not want a cough like theirs, and so Mother said if we take the big umbrella and carry it together then we will not get wet. So you see, sir, we have come to pray and ask Jesus also for rain, and also Mother and Father and sick Aunts can have a little bit of peace and rest while we are in the special prayer meeting. Please, sir, we know you would pray for our need too. Will you pray for our Mother, for she is looking after Daddy and Aunts? We heard our Doctor say to Mummy that they have a T.B. germ. Mummy does not want baby Thelma to pick up any germs."

The Minister, so touched, picked them both up in his arms for they were only little and gave them a big hug and said to all who had come, "A little child shall lead them.

3

Out of the mouths of babes the Lord is praised,' it says in God's word."

The Minister then sat them down in front of him on the smaller chairs. The service commenced, but while they prayed a strong wind arose; the heavens before so bright were now full with clouds. Thunder and lightning followed and then lots and lots of rain just poured down. Those who were not prepared to receive the blessing in faith went home drenched; while the Minister, and little Mary-Flora and young Herbert were taken safely home again sheltered under the great family umbrella! But this was not the 'storm' which was to change our young lives for ever. That storm was getting closer day by day, as yet unseen.

Dear reader, whether you are young or old, let me ask you one question. When you meet with others for prayer, or in the secret of your own room to pray to your loving Heavenly Father, is faith the key which opens your heart before the throne of grace? If not, remember the faith of the children's umbrella; "For we believe God answers prayer, we have proved God answers prayer, glory to His Name!"

The Lord will hear when I call unto Him. Psalm 4 v 3

God is in Heaven; can He hear
A little child like me?
Yes, little child, thou need'st not fear,
He'll listen even to thee.

God is in Heaven; does He care
Thence to send good to me?
Yes, all thou hast to eat or wear,
All God has given to thee.

"God, who giveth us richly all things to enjoy." Timothy 6 v 17

Who holds me with His mighty arm,
And keeps me day by day from harm?
Who guards me while I sleep at night,
And bids me wake with heart so light?

4

Who gives me health and clothes and food
And lets me want for nothing good?
'Tis God, the God who dwells above,
That does it all – for "God is Love".

Who made the sun that shines so bright
And stars that sparkle through the night,
Who made the grass that clothes the ground,
And trees, and flowers that bloom around?

Who made those shining drops of dew,
That rainbow bright, those skies so blue?
'Twas God, the God who dwells above,
That made them all – for "God is Love".

Who gave the blessed Book to me
To tell me what I ought to be?
Who calls a little sinful child,
In words so sweet, and voice so mild?

Who bids me come to Christ to live,
And He will all my sins forgive?
'Tis God, the God who dwells above,
That speaks it all, for "God is Love".

Spring is here! How happy the children were to see the
wild flowers. Down in the meadow, Herbert, and Mary-
Flora, would go, with me in the pushchair. It was quite
safe and the older ones were very fond of gathering flowers.
Herbert and Mary-Flora made daisy chains, and put them
round my neck, for it was safer to leave me in the pushchair
while they picked bunches of primroses and violets from
the meadow away down behind their country cottage in
Wembury, Devon.

Sometimes Mother would push the pushchair that I sat
in, and away down to the meadow they would go. Mother
and the children were delighted to breathe in God's lovely
free fresh air.

One sunny day in spring, Mother with her little ones
took a large box with her. Herbert and Mary-Flora carried

it between them, for Mother had little me in the pushchair. It was not long before I had awakened out of my after lunch nap, so Mother lifted her treasure out and placed me down on a rug in a safe part of the meadow. This time Mother did not take Scottie their pet dog with them, for she and the children wanted to pick as many bunches of flowers as they could.

We all stopped after a while, for Mother wanted to give us all a drink of tea which she had brought with her. We did so very much enjoy the time in the meadow and many were the shouts of joyas they came to brightly coloured clumps of flowers. We went home laden with primroses, violets and daffodils and were able to arrange no less than twenty bunches of flowers. Then Mother and Father would write out a text from the family Bible. They tied a text to each bunch of flowers ready for sick friends around the village, for nearly every village in Devon had many, many T.B. sick patients. The disease, often fatal, had been spread through cows' milk, but nowadays cows are given a test every six months by law. Father suffered from T.B. quite badly himself.

The Minister of the village of Wembury Church had duties which extended far beyond the holding of services. To the village people of Wembury he was a friend and counsellor. Down at the back of our home of this delightful village of Wembury ran the stream. Its waters gently babbled as it ran over the stones. There is an air of serenity about this view of the meadow and the stream in the neighbourhood of our beautiful village, so very typical of the countryside all around in Devon. Wembury, Noss Mayo, Newton Ferrers and other such villages are watered by the River Yealm and owe much of their prosperity to their rich pasturage.

> Cooling the grass in the long summer hours,
> smiling along, smiling along;
> Giving a drink to the birds, and the flowers,
> smiling along, along.

Wider and wider as onward you flow,
rippling along, rippling along;
Carry a blessing wherever you go,
rippling along, along.

Bright little streamlets we children may be,
singing along, singing along;
Loving and helpful, pure hearted, and free
singing along, along.

Chorus:–

Murmuring stream,
Murmuring stream,
Flow to the rolling sea
Murmuring stream
Murmuring stream
Singing of purity.

The stream ran on to the orchard where in the spring
bluebells grew abundantly. In the garden of our village
home lovely roses grew.

Psalm 86 v 5 Thou Lord art good.

See the shining dewdrops
on the flowers strewed;
proving, as they sparkle,
God is ever good,

Chorus:–

Bring my heart thy tribute,
Songs of gratitude,
While all nature utters,
God is ever good.

Hear the babbling streamlet
In the solitude,
With its ripple saying
God is ever good.

See the morning sunbeams,
Lighting up the wood,
Silently proclaiming,
God is ever good.

In the leafy tree-tops,
Where no fears intrude,
merry birds are singing,
God is ever good,

Chorus:–

Bring my heart
thy tribute,
Songs of gratitude,
While all
nature utters,
God is ever good.

CHAPTER TWO

Touches of Bliss

The village of Wembury had a blacksmith, Mr. Coleman. His shop was one of the unchanging features of village life and the smith uses a hand-hammer and variously formed hand tools. He relies on muscular effort in shaping the metal. Although the amount and kind of traffic may change and the number of horses to be shod is not as large as it was in the old days, still there is much for the smith to do. A speciality is the manufacture by hand of shepherds' crooks.

Herbert and Flora would push the pushchair with me in it and away we would go down to see Mr. Coleman the Smith of Wembury shoeing horses. We loved to watch and chatter to him for quite some time. He always had a jar of sweets which he handed out to Herbert and Flora, but to me he would give a lovely piece of toast, toasted specially on his fire which he always had going.

At least once a week an infallible magnet to attract weekly pennies was the Wembury village Post Office shop, before which you would see clusters of sturdy children, toddlers in the charge of capable elder sisters, or brothers all holding on to their money which they had earned by doing small jobs at their homes. All eyes were glued to the shop window.

Herbert and Flora would be seen amongst the other children. Now our mother and father had taught us to be thoughtful to the needs of others, and we would often go on an errand to hand in some tasty things to a sick person from Mother and Father. On the way back the village shop was a big attraction. The shop contained all sorts of foodstuffs, also a thousand-and-one articles as various as can be. Herbert and Flora would ask for the particular sweets they liked.

9

This time they did not spend it all on sweets. "Could we buy a bottle of cough mixture," said Herbert, "we want our Daddy and Aunts to get better for they have got nasty coughs."

From the village of Wembury a journey of five miles would be taken on to Plymouth where Father worked in the Navy. Sometimes he would go out to sea for a few weeks before he was taken ill, but more about this in another chapter.

From Plymouth on to the Tamar Ferry, then into the County of Cornwall, the road to our Grandparents' farm goes on a little way past Saltash. Great treats would be given to us as children, for we were told that Grandad and Grandma would for our birthdays bring out their shire horses to our home in Wembury and take us all the way back to their farm. This of course was a very great thrill for us all and the very, very happy days passed by so quickly.

It was Herbert's birthday on the twenty-first of April, 1935, he was seven. We children would romp and play and sing in our carefree spirits, "Hip, Hip Hoorah! We are off for the day!" Scottie was a great scamp and no sooner had Mother spread the cloth out on the grass under the trees, along would come Scottie and pull the end of the cloth.

Along would come little Flora, now six, with a ball for Scottie to keep him out of mischief, while big brother Herbert would give me a piggy back, and they all would have a romp and play before lunch. Hands clasped all around the picnic cloth we were taught to sing,

Thank You for the world so sweet,
Thank You for the food we eat,
Thank You for the birds that sing,
Thank You, God, for everything. Amen.

The sun shone out brightly, for it was a cloudless morning but it was a little cold, so Grandmother helped Herbert and Flora put on their coats. She also dressed me up well and made sure I was safely strapped in her puschair,

10

for even if a door was left open on the farm sure enough in no time at all, young fifteen month old Thelma would have found her way out, and having a great fascination for water I would find a puddle. I seemed to just love it if it rained and with upturned face would almost drink the rain, as it came out of the heavens.

Herbert had a head of golden curls when he was younger, and very light brown eyes. Flora, a year younger than Herbert, had a lovely dark head of wavy curls. I too had a head of curls and like Flora my eyes were very dark brown which shone out so trustingly. The fresh air out on the farm gave us all a good healthy look and fresh home grown food was eaten with relish. Grandad was getting the shire horses and cart ready for the last trip of that spring holiday to the River Tamar, a most picturesque place, so delightful and peaceful, just around the corner from Saltash where we were on the farm.

Flora would be often seen picking wild flowers and even the occasional poppy; these she would gather and take them in to Grandmother. The shire horses and cart waggon were ready; Grandfather folded the pushchair while Grandmother held me tightly and then with a hand from Grandfather young Herbert and young Flora were helped on to the horse who stood so very patiently. Then came my turn. I almost leaped out of Grandmother's arms into Grandad's arms in excitement.

I was placed safely in the arms of Herbert while Grandad helped Grandmother up with her grandchildren. We were all seated safely. Grandfather loaded the picnic for the day, and also some home baked cakes and fruit for the children. After the trip and holiday we were to arrive home to find our father a very sick man.

CHAPTER THREE

Clouds Thicken

Our father was a Naval Officer based at Plymouth, and in the years long before Mother and Father married, many were the trips that Father had to take to other countries.

Eventually we packed up our picnic things after having spent a most enjoyable holiday in Saltash, never ever forgetting the trip out in a boat with Grandad at the Tamar River. Great excitement there was when Grandad caught some fish.

This trip was quite a change from being on the farm and it all helped to make the most memorable holiday ever spent. The fish were placed in a basket, wrapped in a clean cloth ready to be prepared for their supper when they got back to their home at Wembury, for the whole family were ever so fond of fish.

Grandad lifted Herbert down first and he ran to the back door. He waited, for he could hear Doctor's voice. He had been there for about five minutes outside the back porch, when he felt something cold touch his hand. He was startled and looking down saw their Scottie dog. He appeared to want to get in to lie down by the fire.

Herbert and the dog were great friends, as Herbert on most days would take the pet for a walk. The dog stood on his hind legs and put his forepaws up to the latch as if to say, "Let me in."

"Oh," said young Herbert, "you want to get in do you? You will have to wait just one moment longer while I dry you off." He put the dog's towel on the peg outside the back door, then after hearing the Doctor go out of the front door, Herbert softly opened the back door. He was a very thoughtful lad, though still very young. Through the door, when he opened it, he caught sight of his dear Dad lying in bed downstairs.

His father's face turned towards the open door. His eyes seemed as if they were looking for someone. "Oh, he sees me," Herbert said to himself. "I must bend down and speak to Dad before going into the other room." Herbert certainly did not expect to see his father in a bed downstairs. He shut the door quietly behind him.

"Daddy," he said.

"Hello, my son."

"Dear Daddy, when are you going to get up again? When are you coming round the garden with me and the dog to have a lovely walk together. Are you getting better, Dad?"

The kind hands, so white and thin now, were moving restlessly on the coverlet. Herbert clasped one of the thin hands in his warm hands and stooping down, pressed a warm loving kiss on his father's fingers. He had heard Doctor say that Dad had tuberculosis. It made little Herbert sad to see how thin his father had got. His beard had grown, and his lovely dark eyes looked dull.

Herbert tried to brush away his tears for he had to be a brave boy in front of his younger sisters and said to Mother in a whisper, "Jesus will take care of Daddy, I have asked him to." With that comment Mother gave her big son another embrace and pressed his head close to herself. Then Herbert said, "I think Dad is looking forward to some cooked fish that Grandad caught. Wasn't he clever, Mum? He caught enough for us all."

Mother had set the table and called all her children to sit up. I was placed in my highchair and Grandmother and Grandad sat up at the table in the lovely home of Wembury. This time Flora was asked to thank Jesus for the fish Grandad had caught. She sang, "Thank You for the world so sweet; Thank You for the food we eat; Thank you for the birds that sing; Thank You, God, for everything. Amen."

There was ever so much chatter at the meal table. The children were delighted to tell Mother all about their wonderful holiday on the farm with their Grandad and Grandmother. Grandad, seeing his daughter serving out her

13

husband's meal, offered to take it in to the children's Dad and sit with him for a little while. It was time the children were in bed, but as it was their first night back Mother forgot the time conveniently!

Now young Flora had told Mother quite a lot about the holiday, while Herbert was in with his Dad. So it was Herbert's turn to have his say. "We have done so many thrilling things whilst away on the farm, Mummy," and he tumbled it all out to her.

Herbert, bless him, couldn't know, but soon at seven years of age he was going to have to be the man of the home and help Mother all he could. He would manage it too, for they were taught to be thoughtful children and young Flora would help her Mum wash up and help put the things away. They made sure that their pet dog had enough food and water as well.

While the children were away, three Aunts had gone into hospital for a while, so that evening the Aunts' names were not mentioned and Mother waited for the children to ask for them. Mother was a real dear! Yes, her heart ached, but she had to keep her spirits up for the children's sake though she knew that her sisters did not have long to live.

Now it was getting well past the children's bedtime, and I was rubbing my eyes with one hand and sucking my other thumb. So Mother picked up her little darling, gave me a wash and then carried me up into my cot singing a night prayer. I was asleep before Mother had finished, I was that tired and had had such fun.

Grandad watered and fed his shire horses. He also took the pet dog Scottie out for his last walk of the day to help the little family. By the time he came in, Grandmother had finished her story and really it was well past young Herbert's bedtime, but he had such a lot to tell Mother about the enjoyable holiday.

Grandmother and Grandad kissed their grandson Herbert, and he hugged them and thanked his grandparents for such a happy holiday on the farm. From the window mother and young son Herbert waved to the grandparents

14

as they went down the drive back to their home farm at Saltash.

Now Herbert spent time alone with his mother, which he deserved, for he had been such a dear with his father so ill. He could not do enough for him. Mother sat Herbert on her lap and said, "Tell me all about your holiday." This was wise to take his mind off Father before the young lad's bedtime.

"Oh, Mother," said Herbert, starting right on to the last trip they did on the boat with his Grandad, "Grandmother did not want to go for a trip on the boat. She was not keen on the water, so she had said that we had to enjoy ourselves, while she stayed on the beach with baby Thelma keeping her amused."

Grandmother had had tea with me, as she had packed enough tea for Grandad, Herbert and also young Flora to have their tea on the boat. This would be an extra treat for them to finish off their holiday.

"It was ever so jolly indeed," went on Herbert. "Grandad said there was just enough wind to give a pleasant rocking with an occasional bump into a wave which sent the spray over us. Flora and I were ever so excited! We watched Grandad and one or two others let down the net. Slowly they lowered it and while it dragged behind scooping in the fish at the bottom of the river. They had tea with us in a queer little cabin. Then the net was hauled in and its contents emptied on the deck. The fish jumped, some of them. Flora and I saw lots of wriggling eels with lots of little hurrying scurrying crabs all wanting to get out of the boat. It's a day I will never ever want to forget," Herbert said to Mother." The owner of the boat had said that he would put the boat away until Monday as now it was God's day next day. "He loved God," said Herbert to his Mum, "and I expect he sings with his little family at home just like we do."

CHAPTER FOUR

Pain and Parting

Who shall separate us from the love of Christ? Rom. 8:35

School time came all too quickly after the Easter holidays out on their grandparents' farm at Saltash. It certainly was a holiday to be remembered for a long time. Mother did not have to awaken Herbert and Flora, for they were used to waking early on the farm. She gathered her little treasures around her knee, and commended them to God's care for the day while they were at school, asking Him to help them learn well. They sat down to their breakfast and the hot plate of porridge did them so much good. It certainly strengthened their teeth as it was full of calcium. They were all blessed with lovely sets of teeth. After each meal they would be seen cleaning their teeth well.

With a hug and a goodbye kiss the children went off to the school at Wembury. They met their many school friends again, and each child poured out their stories of what they had done on their Easter holidays. The friends of Flora and Herbert listened with interest to their experiences on their grandparents' farm, and also their trip fishing on the boat. Mother busied herself caring for her little toddler. I was still used to a morning sleep and an after-lunch nap, so there was lots of time Mother could spend with her husband caring for him most tenderly.

The children came back from their first day at school full of the stories of the other friends there. Young Herbert and Flora were ever so hungry. School had worked up such a lovely appetite. This time Mother had cooked one of their favourite meals; home-made stew. It went down a real treat and they came back for a second helping. It did Mother's heart good to see them really enjoying the meal she had cooked, with home grown vegetables from the farm and fresh meat from the butcher.

The children were glad of an early night as they had been quite late the night before, and as they were school days for her two oldest children she liked to keep to regular bedtimes. So, with a story or two, Mother prayed with them and they sang their little evening prayer. She then took them up to their lovely warm beds, for Mother had already placed a hot water bottle in the beds to warm. She kissed each one of her little treasures and for safety took the water bottles down to empty them.

The moon was shining through the windows of the children's bedrooms as Mother entered. Young Flora and I were fast alseep, and in case I would wake up with the full moon shining on our faces she drew the curtains over, to block the bright moonlight out.

That evening, quite late, long after the children had gone to bed, the family doctor arrived at the country home in Wembury. He went with Mother to see her husband. He shook his head when he turned to come away from the sickroom, but kept his thoughts to himself, saying, "May I see the children in bed?" He then went straight up to visit the children.

The doctor enquired for her children and she in reply said that they had had a good first day back at the school after a lovely holiday on the farm at Saltash. He was most interested to hear about the holiday, saying it would have done them the power of good. After hearing about the holiday, he stepped across the landing into the bedrooms. The little girls were fast asleep. He then went into young Herbert's room to look at the sleeping boy.

"We will have to keep a close eye on your children now they are at school again, and especially Herbert. He will still want to have talks with his Dad as he used to when taking the dog out each evening together. Do not stop him, but now I should keep young Flora and wee Thelma away from their Dad's bedroom downstairs. Keep them happily playing when Flora comes home from school, and then she will get so engrossed in what she is doing that her mind will be kept free from worry, for her dad is certainly much worse. I will come in each evening to see your husband and also to enquire after yourself and your son."

Mother always had one of those old-fashioned bowls and jug full of water with soap dish and towel for the doctor to wash his hands after he had examined her husband.

"Have a good night," Doctor said, "and I will send a nurse in each day to help you with the nursing of your husband."

Help was so surely needed for the very sick man, and the nurse was able to turn him and make his bed comfortable. She would also give him a blanket bath for he was too weak to get out of bed now. It was a new nurse who had come to the village of Wembury. She was so kind and helpful and Mother so very much appreciated her help. She was very sympathetic as well when Mother told her that she had just recently lost three sisters, for, as expected, all of them died in the hospital with tuberculosis.

Mother kept her spirits up thinking to herself that her husband was not ill enough to go in hospital, else the doctor would have sent him. In fact he was too ill to move, and Doctor had kept this to himself. Mother had been through far too much already, for a few months ago she had helped nurse her sisters, our Aunts.

Next morning was bright and sunny, and Flora and Herbert ran downstairs and said, "Can we take the dog for a walk before breakfast and before we go to school?" They were up early, and Mother said yes as they had plenty of time. The dog was leaping up and down in excitement hearing the offer to take him out. He was nearly blind now, but he could hear well and he was very well apart from his sight.

Now the children were full of glee, and while they were out one held the lead while the other picked primroses and Devon violets. Then they changed over so the other one could pick some. Between them they picked a lot with as long stems as possible, all neatly arranged so that all Mother would have to do was put them in a vase. They did not want to give Mother extra work. They hurried home to give them to Mother for herself and Daddy.

"You little dears," she said to them, "they really are so lovely, and picked with such loving hands. Thank you, thank you ever so much." She kissed them both and thanked them again for their thoughtfulness. I pulled at Flora's frock to help me with one of my toys which had got stuck, so I was occupied for a little while. Young Herbert carried the vase of flowers into Father's room with Mother opening the door.

"Look at what the children have picked you, dear, before breakfast and before going to school. They were up early so asked to go out, knowing the surprise they were going to bring back. They are so very lovely, aren't they?"

Dad said, "Bless you, my children. That God's blessing may rest upon you, continually, is my prayer for you all," and he placed his hand upon his son's head. With a cheery smile Herbert could smell his breakfast, so said, "Goodbye," to Daddy.

"Do well at school, son", Dad said.

"Bye, Dad. Get better soon and we will have walks together again," came back the reply. With this he was gone, the smell of the food was attracting him now. It was bacon and eggs Mother had cooked for them before going off to school. Mother said grace, and the children gave a hearty Amen. They ate it with relish!

"Thank you, Mum," they said.

"That was delicious," came the comment from Herbert, so very grateful for his meal after the morning walk.

"When you come home from school, my dears, I will have a picnic packed and we can go down into the meadow at the back of our home with young Thelma in the push-chair. A friend is calling to see Dad at that time and we can have tea together in the fresh air."

"Oh Mummy, thank you, thank you!" came the reply from the excited children and even I was excited. They then washed and Mother prayed with them before leaving

19

home for school. "Take care, children, and God bless and keep you safe."

"Bye, Mum, bye, Mum," echoed the children as they went out of the door. Mother waving to them with me in her arms waving also. Mother was able to get most of her work up to date while the two older children were at school. At two o'clock the door-bell rang. It was the friend of the family come to give Mother a chance to get a picnic packed up ready for when the children came home from school.

Mother put the kettle on for a cup of tea which they both had with our sick Dad. He so very much appreciated all that his loving wife was doing for him to try and help get him better. It was four o'clock when the door burst open of the kitchen and in came Flora and Herbert back from school.

"Had a good day?"

"Yes thanks, Mum," replied the children spontaneously. They talked to Mother and the friend for about ten minutes, then Mother put me into the pushchair. The picnic was put in a bag connected to the handle of the pushchair. Flora put the lead on Scottie, their pet dog.

Herbert looked in on his Dad, who by this time had fallen into a refreshing sleep, so Herbert closed the door quietly and went back into the kitchen to tell them. Herbert carried another bag for Mother, with the cups in, and away they went down into the meadow at the very bottom of their back garden, by the stream where it was so peaceful and so very refreshing with the early summer breezes.

With a romp and play with the dog they had real fun. I toddled around trying to catch a butterfly or two, while Mother got tea spread on a cloth under the big oak tree. They stayed out playing for a lovely long time.

"Hush!" said Herbert, "I can hear the cuckoo."

"I love to hear the cuckoo," said Flora. The bird now seemed to be singing all the time, and Mother reminded them of the song,

20

Cuckoo, Cuckoo, pray what do you do?
In April I open my bill,
In May, In May I sing all day
In June I change my tune,
In July, In July away I fly,
In August away I must.

"Has it got a tune?" asked Herbert.

"Yes," said Mother.

"Please teach it to us," said young Flora.

They soon picked up the tune and began to teach it to their friends at school the next day. It was now about time to pack up the picnic things. They had been out for such a long time and they had really enjoyed the time spent in the meadow, and they appreciated all the work that Mother had put in making it such an enjoyable time.

"That home-cooked food was just lovely", said Flora.

"The apples and cheese I think were my favourites," said Herbert. "Mother, have you heard this one? I heard it at school."

"What is it, son?"

"Choose an apple for dessert, friendly apples never squirt juice into your eyes!"

"Very good," said Mother and we all laughed, "quite a poet."

Another romp and a play came before going in for a night bath. I certainly needed a bath for I had tumbled in the grass, rolling over and over and over. Herbert also had lovely dirty knees that could do with a scrub in the bath. Flora loved a hot bath, she would blow bubbles for me. "Again," I said, and again and again I said, so delighted with the lovely colours and giving shrieks of laughter in excitement.

Mother said, "Let's go in now and have those baths before wee Thelma gets too tired."

We were soon in the water really enjoying ourselves. There seemed to be so many shrieks of laughter. Even the dog would prick up his ears as if to say, "I would like to see what they are up to."

"No, you can't go up," said Herbert who was downstairs waiting for his bath. He was amusing himself making a puzzle. The family friend said to Herbert, "I must be off now; tell mother I will be in again very soon."

"Shall I call Mother down"? asked Herbert.

"No, don't do that, Mother has enough to do. Tell her I have put the ironing in the airing cupboard".

"Mother will be pleased, Aunt Betty. Thank you ever so much."

The children called her Aunt, for she was a close friend to the family.

"Bye for now, young Herbert. Help Mother all you can, dear. She tells me all you do for her, and said she has such helpful children."

Herbert smiled and said goodbye. Mother came down with me in her arms. She had put us in our night clothes, as it was not far off bedtime. Into her high-chair she put me who was already asking for a "drink, Mummy."

Flora said, "I will help Thelma with her cup of hot milk, while you go up with Herbert."

Herbert passed on the message from Aunt Betty while he was in the bath. "She's a real dear," said Mother, "I don't know what we would do without all your help. You are all such dears".

Herbert looked up at Mother smiling, so very much appreciating being included in the praise. When they came downstairs, young Flora was reading a bedtime story to me. Flora could read very well, for it was her favourite subject at school. While Herbert was drinking his hot cup of milk, Mother filled the hot water bottles and put them in each bed to warm them before putting the children upstairs.

She had prayers with her little ones before taking them upstairs that night. Flora was ever so tired as well, but she climbed the stairs while Mother carried her youngest charge. She then removed the bottles which had warmed

22

the cot and the bed up well. She cuddled her little daughters and placed me in my cot. Then she tucked young Flora up and she kissed us both and said, "God bless and keep you safe".

By the time she had kissed Flora, I had put my thumb in my mouth and I was away in the Land of Nod, fast asleep. It did not take young Flora long to get to sleep.

Herbert had gone in to see his Daddy while Mother was getting the girls to bed. The window and back door was kept open to get as much fresh air in as possible, for this was all part of the treatment for T.B. Dad coughed an awful lot and Herbert, young as he was, would ask to carry anything for Mother. Often one would come into the father's room to see Herbert bent down by his father's bedside. He was such a comfort to his Dad. Herbert said, "Daddy, will you soon be able to get up?"

"Son, I will never get out of bed again. Soon I am going to be with Jesus, up above the bright blue sky to heaven, where all who have thanked Jesus for dying on the Cross of Calvary for their sins will go to be with Him for ever and ever. Jesus shed His precious blood for us, and this is the only way we can get to heaven. It is by thanking Him for dying and shedding His precious blood for each one of us."

None of us are too young, or too old, dear reader, to come to Him by faith believing and receiving Him into our lives. His Holy Spirit comes into our hearts as a real Person never to leave; and day by day we ask Him to reign in our lives and witness for Him for His glory. *Acts 1 v 8* "Ye shall be witnesses unto Me."

"I'm going up yonder," said Herbert's Dad, pointing straight up to the ceiling. "I'm going to my Jesus." What a change came over his face as he mentioned the wonderful Name of Jesus. Mother came in at this point and beckoned Herbert to come out of the room, but the child's father held on to his hand and he called his wife to come over to him. He kissed his son's hand again and again. "Help

Mother all you can, my dear boy, and may God bless you greatly by winning many souls for Jesus. This is my prayer not only for your Mother, but also for Flora and little Thelma too. 'You see, the Wembury Minister named her 'Thelma' meaning 'The Will of God'. I believe God will help her especially to be a bright witness for Jesus. She is only fifteen months old, but one day she will put her trust in Jesus and thank Him for dying for her sins for herself. Mother will teach you all more about our wonderful Saviour, and continue to go to Sunday School where you will learn very much about Jesus and His love for boys and girls and grown-ups as well."

At this point Mother heard the ring of the door bell, so Herbert said goodnight to Dad and his father replied, "God bless you, my son."

It was the nurse at the door. Mother called her in, and asked Herbert to please give Scottie his evening meal. While Mother talked with the nurse, nurse asked if he was comfortable for the night. Herbert, bless him, remembered that Dad had asked if he could have his bed moved in front of the window, so he told his mother and the nurse at this point.

"Alright, my son," she said, both choking back their tears before Mother went in to sit for a while. Nurse went in to see him as well, but he had gone to sleep.

Herbert said to Mother, "May I get Scottie's red ball over in the opposite meadow? I left it there yesterday."

"Yes, dear, but put something warm on and hurry for it looks as if we could have a shower of rain." Following after Herbert came Scottie.

Mother called, "Put the lead on, Herbert, and keep hold of him," for Scottie was now quite blind but they all loved him dearly. He had good hearing and kept his ears pricked up in case anybody mentioned walks, ball, or bone; then there was great excitement for him.

Herbert found the ball for Scottie as it was his favourite toy. Scottie would carry it in his mouth all the way back home. Of course most of his time now Scottie had to have

24

lead on him when he was out because of his blindness.
Every night Scottie would like the ball placed close to him
in his basket.

It was time that Herbert went to bed as it was getting
late, but he deserved a few privileges. His mother prayed
with Herbert and he also had a bedtime story. Then Mother
went upstairs to tuck him up in his bed. "Goodnight,
Mother," Herbert said.

"Goodnight, my son, and thank you for being such a
great help to me; God will bless you greatly, my dear one."
Mother kissed her son and said she would be up later on.
Mother went quickly downstairs to be with her husband,
and nurse helped move the bed in front of the window, as
this was his wish. Nurse left, and Mother saw her out of
the front door. She went down to the doctor's surgery to
give a report on Father's health for the day. Mother did not
know she was going to do this, so she went back with her
husband who was now very, very ill. She just sat there with
him, with her arm around him for he was sat up with many
pillows because of the awful cough. She prayed much for
him silently and her heart simply ached, but for his sake
and for her little ones, she had to try and put on a brave
face, which was not always easy.

The door bell rang again and this time it was the family
doctor arriving at their home again, as he had promised he
would come. He stayed much longer than usual. He asked
the children's mother if he could go in the children's
bedrooms. This time she did not accompany him. Doctor
then tiptoed across the landing to look at the three children
asleep. He was such a kind fatherly man.

Little Flora and I were fast asleep and like all children,
when they were asleep, I looked quite angelic! He said
under his breath, "God bless these darlings", for he knew
the children's mother had tuberculosis as well. The x-rays
had shown this, but Doctor had to keep this from her, for
she needed all her strength to look after her dying husband
whom she loved so very, very dearly; also special strength

25

was given from on high for looking after these de[a]
treasures.

Into Herbert's room he tiptoed, to find the boy wi[de]
awake, as if he was thinking deeply. "Hello," said Docto[r]
"what is keeping you awake?"

"I just can't get to sleep."

Now the doctor knew that Herbert, with the other ch[il]
dren, was having lots of fresh air and lots and lots of f[un]
over on their grandparents' farm, as well as lots of fun a[nd]
romps in the meadow down by the stream. Such fun
this brings forth healthy sleep. Doctor knew however th[at]
Herbert was very close to his father, and mother had to[ld]
Doctor that her son would say, if she was busy with Flo[ra]
and me, that he was just going in for a short while to ta[lk]
to his Dad. He was concerned to see his father so ill a[nd]
did trust he would be getting better, but now his fath[er]
said he would never get up again and that Jesus was calli[ng]
him away. Yes, it did distress him for he was a loving s[on]
and so very close to them both. If only Doctor could ma[ke]
him better, he would say to Mother. But doctor had do[ne]
and was doing everything in his power to help.

Doctor sat on Herbert's bed. "Please," said Herbe[rt]
"can I get up and have a book to look at and read?"

Doctor, realising what was keeping him awake, reach[ed]
towards the child's bookcase and took out a book of trai[ns]
which would take more than an evening to go through. [He]
sat on the child's bed, for he knew he would be call[ed]
during the evening to go downstairs in to Father's bedroo[m]

It was about an hour later that he heard the childre[n's]
mother call, "Doctor, are you there?"

Doctor said to young Herbert, "You go and look at t[he]
book, and I will come back again before I go". He beam[ed]
down sympathetically at young Herbert then hurried dow[n]
stairs to find that brave father was just passing into t[he]
presence of his Saviour. For does it not teach us in Go[d's]
word those who love Jesus are absent from the body a[nd]
present with the Lord (2 Cor 5 v 8)?

Father was just thirty-eight years old. The doctor stay[ed]

a very long time to comfort our mother who had so very tenderly cared for her dear husband for months. It was going to pull Mother down, for she was far from well herself. She thought her tiredness was because of the extra nursing that she was doing; but Doctor knew different and knowing she was going to need some sleep, he advised her to sleep in Herbert's room. It was obvious what was keeping the young boy from sleeping. He advised the young mother of thirty-one not to tell Herbert that night.

Aunty Betty and the Minister's wife made a cup of tea for them all, for Doctor had 'phoned them earlier to say that if they could call later in the evening, they would be so much needed. The friend of the family, Aunt Betty, took Doctor a cup of tea, with one for Herbert as well. Doctor sat on the bed with him again and said, "We thought a nice hot cup of tea would help you to sleep."

"Oh, thank you," said Herbert to Aunt Betty.

"I promised your mother I would look in this evening." Herbert said to Doctor. "Would you like a biscuit? Mother keeps a tin of them in my drawer just in case I get a bit hungry. It saves me going down after I have been tucked in bed."

"Thank you," said the doctor, "I think I will have one with you," so out got Herbert to pass doctor a biscuit or two. "Chocolate ones are my favourites," said Herbert.

Doctor said, "Now it's time for some sleep, young Herbert," so he tucked the young lad up and gave him a kiss goodnight. With that, Doctor went downstairs and by the time Mother went up young Herbert was asleep, and she bent over her son and gave him a kiss and prayed for God's help over him while he was asleep. Then she went downstairs just to tell them he was sound off.

"I'm so pleased," Doctor said. "Now I will take my leave, but we will have to keep a close eye on young Herbert, Mary-Flora and wee Thelma. 'I'll be in to see you again. Try and take all the rest you can and I would if I were you get some sleep tonight." He looked at her sympathetically, for he knew the shock was going to be too

much. He would have to tell the grandparents that Moth
had only months to live. His heart ached, for this wou
leave the young children as orphans.

CHAPTER FIVE

Left Orphaned

he Minister's wife was a real dear, and she was Mother
nd Father's close friend. She had stayed all night and gave
e young mother and little treasures all the love they
eeded in those hours of calamity. The family doctor had
ld the Minister's wife that Mother was really far from
ell because she has tuberculosis as well. "That is why the
ar soul is getting so tired. She thinks it is because of the
xtra work, and I have let her think this was the reason.
e's been given higher power and strength to care so
onderfully for her beloved husband and little ones."

The beds were made up for the Minister's wife and for
unty Betty, and they all decided to try and get some sleep
the doctor had said this was advisable for them all.
other had been upstairs for about two hours in her bed,
r this was the doctor's wish for her, but young Herbert
ssed and turned. Then he sat up and called to Mother.
e was so pleased to see that she was sleeping in a single
d in his room.

"Hello, Mum," he said. "I've woken up and I just can't
t to sleep again. Can I get up and sit with you?"

Now Mother had brought the kettle up just in case he
oke up, so she switched it on. "Yes," said mother, "that
ight be the best thing for you." Pulling some blankets off
r own bed she wrapped them two or three times round
r young son, and carrying him in her arms went and sat
wn by the window which looked out upon the sea.

The sea had the most glorious sheen of moonlight on it.
Oh, how beautiful," said young Herbert. "We have such
vely views all round our little home, haven't we?"

Mother made a cup of tea for herself and her son. She
as ever so silent, for the scene in Herbert's room, of the
ll moon shining on the water was simply beautiful, and

she always remembered that picture for it was the night h[e] loved one had been called home to Heaven. She kept th[e] thought from Herbert until the next day. With that sh[e] went into the bathroom to have a silent weep. Yes, she w[as] going to miss her husband greatly, for they were ve[ry] devoted to each other and the children. She wiped her ey[e] with the cool flannel, so as not to let her young son see s[he] had been crying.

Herbert had finished his drink of tea when Mother cam[e] back. She had said that they had both better have som[e] sleep, but this time Mother said she would stay in t[he] armchair and drop off to sleep. "My dear child, you c[an] sleep in my arms if you like."

Herbert was so thrilled to have this extra spoiling, a[nd] he needed it. He could feel her heart beating as he press[ed] close to her, and Mother could not hold him tight enoug[h] Choking back her tears in the moonlight she was remind[ed] of that verse in *Deut. 33 v 27* "Underneath are the eve[r] lasting arms." Yes, Jesus was holding them all tight in H[is] everlasting arms and He has promised that "He wou[ld] never leave us nor forsake us". (*Hebrews 13 v 5*).

With a prayer from Mother ascending to our loving Hea[v] enly Father to keep her children safe, she then kissed h[er] young son. Secure in her arms he fell into a deep sleep.

Mother would tell Herbert, and her little daughters t[he] next day after we had had a good breakfast that our Fath[er] had gone to be with Jesus last night.

Safe in the arms of Jesus,
Safe on His gentle breast,
There by His love o'ershaded,
Sweetly my soul shall rest.
Hark! Tis the voice of angels
Borne in a song to me
Over the fields of glory
Over the Jasper Sea.

Chorus:–

Safe in the arms of Jesus,
Safe on His gentle breast,
There by His love o'ershaded,
Sweetly my soul shall rest.

Safe in the arms of Jesus,
Safe from corroding care,
Safe from the world's temptations,
Sin cannot harm me there;
Free from the blight of sorrow,
Free from my doubts and fears;
Only a few more trials,
Only a few more tears.

Jesus, my heart's dear refuge,
Jesus has died for me;
Firm on the Rock of Ages
Ever my trust shall be;
Here let me wait with patience,
Wait till the night is o'er;
Wait till I see the morning
Break on the golden shore.

The next day and days to come were to be very busy
ones. Mother, Aunt Betty (our friend), and the Minister's
wife were wonderful to the fatherless children and we were
constant friends to our mother who loved and cared for her
children so dearly.

We were awake early, so Mother washed and dressed
me, gave a book to Herbert and Mary-Flora and said, "Why
not read your books together on the carpet in the front
bedroom." Mother did not want them to go downstairs
without her that day. "I won't be long washing and dressing
Thelma," said Mother, "then you can use the bathroom
after I have finished, Flora dear. Afterwards you can let
Herbert have the bathroom, and I can see you in the kitchen
and do your hair before Herbert comes down. You can play
with your young sister until I have got the bacon and eggs
ready." They will need a good hot breakfast, she thought
to herself.

It was not long before Herbert was down, ever eager to enjoy his Mum's cooking. "It smells good, Mum, and I can hardly wait to start eating."

"Well, son, you had better say grace for us today as you are so very eager to start."

"Thank you, loving Heavenly Father, for our lovely food provided. Amen."

Now they had just finished their cups of tea when the door-bell rang. "I wonder who it could be coming so very early," said young Herbert. But Mother, knowing who it was, got up quickly to let Doctor in before surgery. Doctor was given a chair to sit on and Mother gave the Minister's wife a chair, also their friend was given one as well. Mother lifted me out of her high chair and sat me on her lap. The Minister's wife took young Flora on her lap and the doctor sat Herbert on his knee.

'Shall I go and get my train book?" asked Herbert, thinking the doctor had come to finish looking through his train book with him.

"You may, if you like," said Mother, "but come right back into the kitchen with it, for Doctor will have to do surgery when the time comes".

"I will be as quick as lightning," said Herbert.

"All right, let's see. We will time you," said Doctor, making a game out of it. Herbert soon came back with his train book, and Doctor drew him on his knee again, for he was going to need to feel his strong arms around him before long. Now, Mother asked, could the Minister's wife pray and ask for God's help throughout the day.

"Yes gladly." She was so very tender in her prayer for them all, and our loving Heavenly Father certainly helped the young Mother of thirty-one years to tell her little ones. She said, "Herbert, my dear," and young Flora and I listened as well from Mother's lap, "your Daddy went to be with Jesus last night".

Herbert, from the Doctor's knee, spoke up and said, "He was going away to be with Jesus and he said we were to be good children and help Mother all we could."

32

"Well," said Mother, "you said Daddy had told you a few days ago that he would be taken to be with Jesus, and last night he was taken".

"Yes, he has gone away," said Herbert. "And he's not coming back again and we liked him so much," he sobbed. "My Daddy, my dear, dear Daddy's gone, what shall we do without him".

"Don't cry, Herbert," said little Flora, not realising her father had been so very ill, for during each day Mother made sure to keep Flora out of her Daddy's room and gave her toys so she could play with me. "Don't cry," said Flora again. "I will go and find him. Daddy's gone in the garden I expect". But with that Mother said that Daddy was now in Heaven with Jesus. "He will be free from pain".

"Yes," sobbed Herbert, "he's above the bright blue sky, so we can't get him back again, Flora." With this they all sobbed and sobbed their little hearts out. I started to suck my thumb and held on to my Mummy, quietly sobbing.

What a kind doctor he was. He also knew that Herbert would be only eight years old when his Mother would be taken to be with Jesus. Flora would then be seven.

"We will look after you," Doctor promised, "and we also know that our loving Heavenly Father will care for you and meet your every need."

Doctor had a talk with the Minister on the 'phone when he went back to the surgery, and was heard to say. "Those dear little children and mother are so in need of comfort and help. You see, I only give the mother months to live".

"Really?" said the Minister.

"Yes, really. She has been wonderful, and she certainly has been given strength from on high to cope with nursing her beloved husband and caring for her children. She will go down hill quickly now, I'm afraid to say."

Tragedy increased for the family when Grandmother died after a very short illness, and Mother's health deteriorated rapidly. Doctor called frequently, but more and more Mother was forced to take to bed, and Aunt Betty cared for the many needs. Inevitably the crisis day approached and after a particularly bad night Mother's strength seemed to have all but gone. The children were prepared and sent to school for their minds needed to be occupied. It was going to be such a heartbreaking day for them, and they were going to need their friends at school to play with now, and in future days as well.

Mother watched from her home window as the young children left with Aunt Betty the family friend to go to school. She lingered long, watching and waving to her treasures until they were out of sight. With a sigh she sat down and was heard to say, "Life's day is short, I soon shall go to be with Him who loved me so; I see in the distance that shining shore." With this Mother held out her arms to hold Thelma – me, her baby of eighteen months.

Doctor advised the young mother to lie down once Aunt Betty had come back from taking the children to the village school at Wembury. This she was very glad to do, as by this time she had become so very weary. Doctor said goodbye and said he would be in after surgery. Aunt Betty took me twelve o'clock lunch. I was washed after lunch, and played with my toys happily while the washing up was being done.

Now it was while I was having my afternoon sleep that the doctor called. Both Aunt Betty and the doctor went into Mother's bedroom. It was about two o'clock. Doctor sat on one chair and Aunt Betty sat by Mother holding her hand. About half-past-two our brave mother, who had been through so much, was called home to be with Jesus in Heaven.

There was such a lot to do before the older children came home from school. Placed on the table by the bed, where Mother used to rest, was this poem and a note for Herbert and Flora. "Be good children, my darlings, and take good care of your baby sister Thelma." With tear drops on the letter and poem, written down for her children to read, was the prayer of the last verse, "Oh, Jesus, strengthen my darlings while here, and keep them in Thy loving care until we see Thee face to face and each other's face again. Amen.

I am going to be with Jesus, See you soon, my treasures. All my love, from your darling Mother."

She knew she would be called to Heaven before they came home from school. There was heartbreaking sobbings from the three orphans when Mother died of tuberculosis. We had been through so much.

Walking along life's road one day,
I heard a voice so sweetly say,
A place up in Heaven I am building thee,
A beautiful, beautiful home.

Loved ones upon that shore we'll meet,
Casting our crowns at Jesus' feet.
We'll worship and praise Him for evermore,
In our beautiful, beautiful home.

Life's day is short I soon shall go,
To be with Him who loved us so.
I see in the distance that shining shore,
Our beautiful, beautiful home.

Fallen asleep,
Lying at rest,
Tranquil and deep,
Safe on His breast!
Life's journey o'er,
Heaven's portal passed,
Pilgrim no more,
Safe home at last!
Safe home at last!

No more to fear,
No more to die,
Shed every tear,
Breathed every sigh!
All sorrows borne,
All trials past,
No more to mourn,
Safe home at last!
Safe home at last!

Gone home to be with Jesus,
Away from toil and care,
Gone home to be with Jesus,
The crown of life to wear.

Gone home to be with Jesus,
Her saviour, guide and friend
Gone home to share the joy and peace,
That ne'er will know an end.

Gone home to be with Jesus,
How sweet, how blessed, how grand.
To think she's safely landed,
In fair Immanuel's land!

The parting may be bitter,
The trial may be sore,
But oh, how sweet it is to know,
She's only gone before!

Her fight on earth is ended,
Her work of love is done.
And Jesus took her home to be
With Him, beyond the sun.

She's heard the call and entered in,
She's seen her Saviour's smile.
And sweet to think we'll meet again,
In but a little while.

Yes, meet again to part no more,
In that bright land above.
And there we'll meet all those we know,
And Jesus, whom we love.

Then how this thought should brighten,
And make us strive to be,
More like our Saviour and our King,
Whose face we then shall see.

Oh, Jesus, strengthen us while here,
And help us in the fight,

Until we see Thee face to face,
Thou blessed lamb of light.

We are waiting for the moment
That is ever drawing nigh,
To be caught up all together,
And to meet our Lord on high.

We shall see Him and be like Him
Nevermore to fail and die.
For He'll change these feeble bodies
In the twinkling of an eye.

The Power Of Prayer

There is an eye that never sleeps
Beneath the wing of night.
There is an ear that never shuts,
When sink the beams of light.

There is an arm that never tires,
When human strength gives way;
There is a love which never fails
When earthly loves decay.

But there's a power which man can wield,
When mortal aid is vain
That eye, that arm, that love to reach,
That listening ear to gain.

That power is prayer, which soars on high.
Through Jesus to the throne,
And moves the hand which moves the world,
To bring salvation down.

Jesus Christ the same, yesterday and today, and for
ever.

Hebrews 13 v 8

CHAPTER SIX

Hospital Experiences

When my brother Herbert was eight years old, and my sister Flora was seven and I was just eighteen months, the three of us were left as orphans. How blessed it is to know that when sorrow or sickness comes into a home, and the children are left as orphans, that our loving Heavenly Father knows and loves and cares for us and wants to draw us closer to Himself.

Precious promises from our loving Heavenly Father given to us from His most precious Book the Holy Bible. "As one whom his mother comforteth, so will I comfort you". Also in *Psalm 27 v 10*, "When your father and mother forsake you, then the Lord will take you up."

At this early age, when Father and Mother and all the adults had died we were, after much prayer, from the Minister and his wife of Wembury, taken to a Christian orphanage in Bristol known as Müller's Orphanage at Ashley Down, where we were *well* cared for in every way.

These five large buildings, built through answers of prayer, show our loving Heavenly Father's great faithfulness to us. These buildings stand as an inspiration to many thousands all around the world who daily thank our wonderful Heavenly Father for meeting the needs of the orphans.

When we were examined, my brother was found to have a spot on his lung and so he went to Hawkmoor Hospital, Moretonhampstead in Devon. I was found to be walking sideways, holding on to everything, and appeared to be in much pain at the age of eighteen months. A letter was written to our doctor to find out if I had had my triple injection for whooping cough, tetanus and diphtheria. The reply came back to say that I had, so now I was given a very thorough examination and x-rays proved that I had caught tuberculosis of the spine, which had been passed on to me through my mother's milk. So I was carried by Sister Duker into an ambulance which had been sent to take me to Frenchay Hospital, Bristol.

There, for the next four years I was put in a tilted cot, with my head often downwards and my feet were put in traction. The second day I was wheeled into a brightly painted room and sat in a large golden armchair where the sun shone in through the window. I remember it as a great comfort to me, as a very little child who had not long lost my mother. You can imagine the loss of my mother was very great, as I was in pain as well. Now, in the brightly lit room (to have a new dress, no!) at the age of two years, Mr. Priddy, my surgeon from Frenchay Hospital said I was to have plaster-of-paris all over my body.

This plaster-of-paris was renewed as I grew, so from two years until six, off and on I would be put into that same golden armchair in the brightly lit room to await another plaster-of-paris. Once the plaster-of-paris was arranged to be changed when I had a birthday, and I sat on the floor of the ward and opened the lovely gifts which kind friends had sent in for me.

When I had my first Plaster-of-Paris put on at two, the warmth of it going on my body was a great comfort to me, for I did so miss the warmth of being held by my mother. Before I was put in my hospital cot for four years, missing my mother greatly and my brother Herbert and my sister Flora, the only thing which seemed to belong to me was my thumb which I found such great comfort in sucking. As I said, my body was covered with plaster-of-paris and often my head was tilted downwards. This poem is so apt here:–

Thelma was so very ill

Thelma was so very ill,
But God remained all faithful still,
From orphan home and hospital,
Prayer, faith and love will yet prevail.

Whenever friends and teachers came,
To sit with her awhile,
They always found, despite the pain,
Face bright with sunny smile.

My Lord, dost Thou indeed remember me,
Just me, the least and last,
With all the names of Thy redeemed,
And all Thy angels has it seemed,
As though my name might perhaps be overpassed;
Yet here I find Thy word of tenderest grace.
True for this moment, perfect for my case –
Thus saith my Saviour, "I remember you."

Sister Duker would carry me around before going to
spend the four years in my new cot, and she seemed to
understand my need of a mother's arm around me, and she
comforted me greatly in my sobs. Hearing I was missing
Mother and brother, my sister Flora told the kind friends
in Muller's Orphanage that we used to have a pet black
Scottie dog in our home at Wembury. So with kind gifts
the friends sent in a toy black Scottie dog for me.

We were nursed out of doors in our cots day and night
by kind nurses and doctors. My loving Heavenly Father
gave me lots of new friends, and I cannot thank Him
enough. Many of the children in hospital would come and
talk to me in the day, for they were allowed to get up.
Before they sat around for school in hospital, they would
bring me toys and books to look at while lying on my back.

Little Rosemary came into our ward one day. She was
in such great pain. Her body was broken in a car accident.
One night it was wet, cold and frosty, and so our cots and
beds stayed in. Although I could not see little Rosemary
from the position I was in, I could hear her talking to the
friend by her. Little Rosemary said, "Each night, Jesus'
angel comes through the ward; the lights are left on low all
night, but in case I have fallen asleep, please tell Jesus'
angel that I am the next one to be taken to Heaven."
Rosemary's body was racked with pain. Rosemary said to

her little friend in the bed next to her, "Tell Jesus' angel I will be the little girl with my hand and arm up on my pillow. This way he will not miss taking me next."

During the night Jesus did take little Rosemary's spirit to be with Himself. "Safe in the arms of Jesus". How very happy to know that there is a friend for little children above the bright blue sky.

On my fourth birthday I had a birthday cake made in the hospital. Great care was taken of me as they lifted me out of my cot every birthday. Each year for my birthday in Frenchay Hospital, Bristol, the friends in the orphanage sent me in gifts. Also at Christmas I can well remember some of the gifts sent in for me: a doll, books, a box of bricks. For these acts of kindness, and for the faithful visits from Sister Duker, Miss Scott, Nurse Weazner, Miss Hickford, Miss Kemp, Miss Sweeting, Miss Grace Morwood and others, I shall always be grateful.

As a little orphan I used to thank all those dear people who sent in gifts of money for my toys and clothes. May I again, from the bottom of my heart, thank you for your labours of love; no expense was spared to get me better. The Directors, Mr. and Mrs. Green, Mr. and Mrs. Tilsley and Mr. and Mrs. McCready would call all the staff to pray for my recovery. They prayed for me mornings, two o'clock and also each evening. Before going to bed you would see all the orphans kneeling by their beds to pray for me. In such very loving ways my loving Heavenly Father cared for me. *Matthew 18 v 10*.

It was Sunday morning and already, although so young, it was becoming my favourite day. From my hospital cot I was not able to look around and therefore could not see what was going on. I used to love to lie there, and on Sunday mornings my heart used to leap in anticipation as I waited to hear the Salvation Army playing their instruments and singing their heart-felt praises to our loving Heavenly Father, for Jesus His precious Son. They would come right outside our ward and play and sing many old favourite hymns.

All things bright and beautiful,
All creatures great and small,
All things wise and wonderful,
The Lord God made them all.

Each little flower that opens,
Each little bird that sings,
He made their glowing colours,
He made their tiny wings.

The purple headed mountain,
The river running by,
The sunset and the morning,
That brightens up the sky.

The cold wind in the winter,
The pleasant summer's sun,
The ripe fruits in the garden,
He made them every one.

He gave us eyes to see them,
And lips that we might tell,
How great is God Almighty,
Who hath made all things well.

Also:–

Rock of Ages cleft for me,
Let me hide myself in Thee;
Let the water and the blood
From Thy riven side which flowed,
Be of sin the double cure,
Save me from its guilt and power.

Also:–

There is spring time in my soul today,
For when my Lord is near,
The Dove of Peace sings in my heart,
The flowers of grace appear.

Chorus:–

Oh, there's sunshine, blessed sunshine,
When the peaceful, happy moments roll;
When Jesus shows His smiling face,
There is sunshine in my soul.

Also:–

There is a green hill far away,
Without a city wall,
Where the dear Lord was crucified,
Who died to save us all.

These lovely hymns and others that they played and sang
were going to keep ringing in my ears over the years I was
to stay in Frenchay Hospital.

I was born on a Sunday morning, 1934, and a Sunday
morning everywhere seemed even more peaceful than other
days and I just loved the sound of the birds singing their
notes of praise to our loving Heavenly Father.

God's eye is on the sparrow.

When the birds begin to worry
And lilies toil and spin,
And God's creatures all are anxious,
Then I also may begin.

For my Father sets their table,
Decks them out in garments fine,
And if He supplies their living,
Will He not provide for mine?

Just as noisy, common sparrows
Can be found most anywhere;
Unto some just worthless creatures,
If they perish who would care?

Yet our Heavenly Father numbers
Every creature great and small,

43

Caring even for the sparrows,
Marking when to earth they fall.

If His children's hairs are numbered,
Why should we be filled with fear?
He has promised all that's needful,
And in trouble to be near.

Take heart, dear child of God. Our loving Heavenl<
Father knows your need and He will provide for ever
need. Just keep trusting and praising Him for all His grea
love.

It was getting towards my fifth birthday, and we childre
looked forward to our birthdays in the hospital. Ther
would always be a birthday cake of some sort. I can wel
remember gifts being sent in for me. These kind gifts wer
sent in to me from friends at the Orphanage, and my hear
was truly thankful to them all. My brother Herbert an
sister Flora would send me a birthday card and a gift.
just longed to see my brother and sister, but in those day
children were not allowed to visit sick ones in hospital. I
was lovely though when I had a letter from them.

Dear friends abroad in America and other parts of th
world, and also friends from England, thank you for you
kind gifts and for your very faithful prayers which wer
truly valued and so very much appreciated. With true grati
tude I would like to thank you all from the bottom of m
heart. I would not have pulled through that big operation
nor the four and a half years in a spika frame covered a
over with plaster-of-paris, had you not prayed for me s
faithfully.

My loving Heavenly Father sent His angels to care fo
me all the time. How do I know? In Matthew 18 v 1(
"For I say unto you, that in Heaven their angels do alway
behold the face of My Father which is in Heaven."

My surgeon, named Mr. Priddy, from Frenchay Hospit
sent a letter to the Directors and Dr. Burgin in Muller
Orphanage to say that my spine was going to have to b
operated on. You see, when I was in hospital at that tende

44

early age, they did not have streptomycin to give, so my treatment for tuberculosis of the spine was rest and fresh air. Day and night our cots, and older ones in their beds, would be put outside the ward.

After some years of this treatment, x-rays showed it was not getting better and pus was building up in my groin. Quick attention needed to be taken if my life was to be spared. The Directors signed the operation form, for a big operation was going to be the only thing that Mr. Priddy my surgeon could do for me. My life was certainly going to be in his hands, and I cannot thank him enough for the great care he took on me while in Frenchay Hospital.

After the form was signed, I was for one of the last times lifted out and put in the golden chair, which was in the bright sunny room. It really was so pleasant in the room, and the joy of sitting in the chair for just a short while was a privilege I shall never forget.

The Directors asked all the staff of the Orphanage to pray for me. This they did constantly throughout each day, and especially again each afternoon at two o'clock. The staff of the Muller Homes still gather for prayer every day at this hour, to pray for the work, needs, and sick ones. The children all prayed too; hundreds of them, a sight to behold, to see so many orphaned children praying and kneeling by their beds in believing prayer. God bless them all for their very faithful prayers.

It was two o'clock on a September day, 1938, when Mr. Priddy gathered his staff together at Frenchay Hospital. He was a kind family man with a number of sons. He, too, wanted this operation to be successful and while the Directors, Sister Duker, staff and children prayed at the Müller Orphanage, God's higher more skilful hand was placed over the surgeon's while he performed the operation. Unseen by the human eye, my loving Heavenly Father guided the surgeon's hands. Yes, I was as it were a lump of clay in the Heavenly Potter's hands.

45

He shapeth at the potter's wheel,
The vessel He hath planned,
My little mould of human clay,
Is in His mighty Hand,
We durst not tell Him what to do,
Nor should we doubt His skill;
But wholly yield ourselves to Him,
To work His perfect will.

He worketh at the potter's wheel,
He worketh night and day;
With patience inexhaustable,
He fashioneth the clay
And from that crude and shapeless lump,
Within His Hands' embrace,
A work is wrought upon the wheels
Of glory, and of grace.

He riseth from the potter's wheel,
His workmanship complete
And lifteth in His skilful Hands
The vessel, trim and neat.
With admiration and delight
He setteth it aside –
Meet only for the Master's use,
In honour to abide.

'Tis thus that God does work in us
That perfect work begun,
And will perform it till we bear
The image of His Son.
When in the glory of His house,
Each vessel will display,
The wonders of His matchless grace
For ever and for aye.

Jeremiah 18 v 3 "Behold, He wrought a work on wheels."
Ephesians 2 v 10 "We are His workmanship."
2 Timothy 2 v 21 "A vessel unto honour, sanctified and
meet for the Master's use."

Placed on a hospital trolley before my operation, big brown saucer eyes showed my fear of the unknown. It was such a big operation which was to take many hours. I well remember a nurse kindly held my hand in comfort, and I was asked to breathe in chloroform for the anaesthetic. I remember, too, the cover being put over my head. The nurse was a sweet person, and she held my hand while she prayed for me. She told me also I would go off into a nice long sleep. Before going into the operating room, back in Mullers I was constantly being prayed for. I was on the danger list for many months, and had to be in a room on my own. I was not left alone at all, for I was so ill;

We cannot always understand
The things which God for us hath planned,
His sovereign ways, past finding out,
May cause the anxious heart to doubt,
Yet in the end 'tis plain to see
That He hath dealt most graciously.

Doth He not know the way we take?
Doth He not care? Would He forsake
A suffering one for whom He died?
Ah no! His promises abide,
For ever sure! They cannot fail,
Though fears and foes the heart assail.

Thus, as we cringe beneath the rod,
And feel forsaken of our God,
At last, in piteous, tender love,
He lifts the rod and from above,
Sends sweet relief – the trial o'er
The gold shines brighter than before.

"He measured and brought me through" Ezekiel 47: 3 & 4

That weakness and pain so hard to bear,
That sorrow and trial too,
It did not last – it passed away
He measured – and brought me through.

Not a moment too long did it remain,
Though 'twas hard to bear 'tis true,
But there came an end with a spiritual gain,
He measured and brought me through.

In a wonderful way He revealed Himself
In a way entirely new,
As Jehovah-Ropheca I knew Him then,
He measured and brought me through.

'Tis always so with our Loving Lord,
Be the trials many or few,
He times them all – His appointed time,
He measures and brings us through.

Child of God in trial, it soon will end,
Trust Him for His word is true;
Be patient and wait, in His own good time
He will measure and bring you through.

Sister Duker, S.R.N. now came to call for me, to take
me back to Muller's Orphanage to be nursed by her in the
infirmary by day. At night in the infirmary at Mullers a
night nurse was provided for me called Nurse Weazner.
They cared for me as if I was their own child.

I missed the company of the children from Frenchay
Hospital for I had made so many friends there. It had
become my second home, as I was there for four and a half
years and I cannot speak too highly of the tremendous care
and love I received from the nurses and doctors. Great
gratitude from the depths of my heart goes out to Mr.
Priddy my surgeon.

Because I missed my friends so much, Sister Duker asked
if Violet could come up to the infirmary to be my friend,
and she has been my friend ever since that day. We had
great fun together. One day I can recall that the pet kitten
went missing. Where could it be? It was missing for days.
We always, each day, had a thanking prayer to our loving
Heavenly Father and an asking prayer, after thanking God
for all His great love toward us in giving us food and shelter

each day and safety at night. We then in our prayers began to ask our loving Heavenly Father, "Please could our little tabby kitten be kept in safety and please could he come back to us again."

Day after day we prayed and then on the seventh day, it was a Saturday, in walked Alexander our pet kitten. How we children thanked our loving Heavenly Father for taking care of him and sending him back to us again.

A new friend came up to the infirmary. She was called Margaret. Margaret was a year older than I was, but she had caught chicken-pox and so it was not long before Violet and I got it as well! Violet was so pleased I remember, because this meant she did not have to go down to her school lessons and was able to play with me all day. When Violet and Margaret and other children got better from their chicken-pox they then had to go down with the hundreds of other children. I was not allowed to go down with the other children for a long, long time, so I was often alone with Sister Duker. My thick leather jacket only came off for baths, and Sister Duker was the only one who took it off and put in on after she had bathed me. I even slept in the jacket for a few years.

For the great care she took of me, and tender love she showed to us all, I will never be able to thank her enough. I cannot speak too highly of the loving devotion she showed toward me personally. I slept in a little cot, for a cot was safer for me in case I fell out of bed. It was when I was first put in a bed that I woke up out of it with my pillow on my back. I had been found in one of the dormitories. A kind teacher, Miss Scott, with Miss Foreshaw took me back to the infirmary.

Each day Sister Duker started to teach me Psalm 23 which has been and always will be a great comfort to all sick ones. This psalm has been a great help to people all round the world. Sister Duker would read Psalm 23 through a few times first, then verse by verse I would learn it. You see, now I did not have my mother's knee to stand by and learn such precious truths.

49

"The Lord is my Shepherd; I shall not want (Psalm 23)
"He maketh me to lie down in green pastures" (rest);
"He leadeth me beside the still waters" (drink);
"He restoreth my soul" (forgiveness);
"He leadeth me in the paths of righteousness'
    (guidance);
"For Thou art with me" (company);
"Thy rod and Thy staff they comfort me" (comfort);
"For Thou preparest a table before me" (food);
"My cup runneth over" (joy);
I shall not want:– in this life,
For goodness and mercy shall follow me
All the days of my life.
I shall not want – anything for the life to come
"For I will dwell in the house of the Lord for ever."

Dear reader, no man or woman has ever suffered like my precious Lord and Saviour Jesus Christ did for you and me on Calvary's Cross. Jesus said that out of pity for us He would bear the punishment instead.

"Lift up thine eyes on yonder rugged tree, and there behold the dying agony of One, the Son of God; was ever pain like this? Who for thy welfare did sustain the pangs of Calvary, the piercing thorn, the cruel nails, the gibing and the scorn of wicked men assembled there below – who suffered thus because He loved you so, and bearing all your sin upon the tree, did make a full atonement there for thee."

CHAPTER SEVEN

Prayer and Care

The young Prussian student from Halberstadt came to England with hardly a penny. He chose Wilson Street, St. Pauls, in Bristol as the spot to open his first orphan house. As his family grew, there were complaints from neighbours about the noise at play hours. It helped to make up George Müller's mind to move. Ashley Down, Bristol's open country, then caught his eye.

The story of how he bought the land and built the Orphanage's empire on the power of prayer is too well known to repeat in detail. The Müller statistics still make remarkable reading. His five large orphan homes cost £115,000 and accommodated 2,050 orphans. During George Müller's life 10,000 orphans passed through his hands and cost him nearly a million pounds *and all raised by prayer*. George Müller *never* made a public appeal for cash nor have the men who followed him. When I was there as an orphan I had the privilege of looking after the Directors and staff of the corridor, and providing trays of tea for them.

The trustee prayer meetings were a great inspiration to me as well, for when I knocked at the door to take in tea for them all, thinking on one occasion that I heard someone say come in, I opened the door quietly to see with my very own eyes forty godly men all kneeling down around a great oblong table seating twenty each side.

These men of God were praying to our loving Heavenly Father in the Name, that precious Name of our Lord and Saviour Jesus Christ. They were praying for the needs of the orphans and thanking Him for the answers of many prayers on our behalf. All the Directors, their wives and staff amounting to more in number than the trustees, meet

51

in George Müller's old study for an hour of prayer each day at two o'clock.

When I hear from them, they often make mention that they have been praying for me. Never will I forget their very faithful prayers on my behalf as a little girl on the danger list for many years suffering from a T.B. spine. I almost lost my life during the operation Mr. Priddy the surgeon did on my spine and groin. We truly needed so very much the prayers of the staff of the orphanage. Every child was taught to pray by their beds in the morning and before getting into bed at night. We surely needed to pray, for we had many needs, being orphaned in our very early childhood.

I believe God answers prayer,
I am sure God answers prayer.

When I was in the Müller's Orphanage, Ashley Down, Bristol, it was always a hive of industry. 2,000 orphans rose at 6.00 a.m. asking God to keep us safe, for these were War days, and asking Him to help us with our lessons each day. These began with morning assembly at 9 o'clock.

Having had T.B. of the spine I was given a mug of cold milk at 11 o'clock and a hot mug of milk at night before bed. In the afternoons, for an hour, we girls would knit our winter stockings and would also knit the younger girls' stockings and some vests. We were also taught to do beautiful embroidery, also marking.

The boys had their separate orphanage. No. 4 was their home. The boys, if they had sisters, only saw them to talk to once a month, but nowadays I'm so very pleased to say that brothers and sisters grow up together in the same home. I'm so pleased that they are not separated now, because when I was nine and out of the Infirmary of Müllers, but still wearing the thick leather spinal jacket, the teachers said I often sleep walked. They would lead me back to my bed, but sometimes I would wake up in a friend's bed in the girls' dormitory. After a while I would come to, and realise that I was not in my own bed because I would have my shoes on!

One day, when I was nine, the older girls said we were going for a long walk and this time we were going to visit a church. I was never allowed to do long walks, but the older girls would give me piggy backs. To them I was not heavy – I was their friend! On this particular day though, my heart really leapt with joy for I overheard some of the older girls say that in the church there would be "Mummies". They meant, of course, the mothers with their children who lived in the houses locally, who would also be at the service.

I immediately thought at last I would be able to see my mother, and when we arrived at the church my heart so ached for nobody had ever told me, and I had never seen "Mummies" in a church before. Hence the sobs started all over again, and the sleepwalking continued for a few years, at least till after the War. I had gone through so very much at such an early age. How I used to pray for God's help.

When I was nine, after kneeling by my bed one night, I got into bed, covered my head with my sheet and just cried and cried to my loving Heavenly Father, saying, "Please, Heavenly Father, You have taken my Mother and Father. I miss them so very much; please, oh please, send me help."

My friend Violet was told I was crying. She had been my friend since I came out of hospital at six and a half years of age. Violet was three months older than I was. She had three sisters and four brothers in Müllers, for their parents had died in Cornwall.

God did answer my prayers, for Violet and I opened our Bibles and in bold letters *John 14v18* leapt right out of the page, and my loving Heavenly Father gave me the promise, "*I will not leave you as orphans, I will comfort you.*" From that day on I knew that my very loving Heavenly Father was never going to leave me nor forsake me (*Hebrews 13v5*), for He had given me this promise. His wonderful word is just full of promises and He's a faithful God and never breaks His promises.

The War was still on and I was ten in 1944. I had not been at all well and so was being nursed in the Orphanage infirmary. The Sunday before I went into the infirmary, two Canadians came to give us God's message in the Gospel that day. The lights were all put out and the platform was floodlit. There was a very large screen, and while the husband sang a piece called "In the Garden of Gethsemane", the wife drew in chalks our precious Saviour in the Garden.

The Canadian then told us the full Easter story. It so gripped me I shall never ever forget it. After that Sunday and during that same week I was sent up to the infirmary with Sister Duker. One night I was running a temperature and I had a dream. It was two o'clock in the morning, so it was pitch black yet the whole ward lit up and in my dream which was so real my Lord was in bright white garments. He was climbing Calvary's Hill with His cross. The Lord was speaking to my soul and continued to do so until September 16th, 1944 on a Friday afternoon, when Violet and I knelt down. I was ten and I thanked Jesus from the bottom of my heart for dying on the cross of Calvary for my sins, and I truly thanked Jesus for His precious, precious blood that He shed for me.

There is power in the precious blood of Jesus and it is our only passport to Heaven; will you not thank Jesus for dying on Calvary's Cross for your sins?

In *Revelation 3v20* Jesus said, "Behold I stand at the door and knock. If any man hears My voice and opens the door, I will come in to him and will sup with him and he with Me".

We sang this hymn on that Sunday morning when those Canadians came to give God's message to us.

There is a Fountain Filled with Blood

There is a fountain filled with blood,
Drawn from Immanuel's veins,

54

And sinners plunged beneath that flood,
Lose all their guilty stains.

The Chorus says:—

I do believe, I will believe,
That Jesus died for me,
That on the Cross He shed His blood,
From sin to set me free.

E're since, by faith I saw the stream,
Thy flowing wounds supply,
Redeeming love has been my theme,
And shall be till I die.

'Tis Jesus only – Matthew 17v8

"Jesus only", – let me see Him, in the glory of His
  grace,
With the eye of faith behold Him, and to look upon
  His face,
Where the glory of the Father, doth in radiant splendour
  shine,
Oh, to turn my eyes in wonder, on that countenance
  divine!

"Jesus only" 'Twas the Saviour, in the days of long ago
Who did manifest His glory, and His majesty did show;
When His visage was transfigured, and His raiment
  shone as light
Oh, to stand upon the mountain, and behold that
  wondrous sight!

The things of earth receded, as the light of glory shone,
From the countenance of Jesus, Heaven's beloved one,
No other man was sighted, every eye was turned on
  Him,
Oh, to look at Jesus only, while the things around grow
  dim!

"Jesus only" – I shall see Him, in that bright and
  blessed place,

And will gaze in silent wonder, at the beauty of His
   face,
As the little ones adored Him, when they gathered
   'round His knee,
So my heart will be enraptured, when my Saviour's face
   I see.

Jesus' Footprints

*One night a man had a dream. He dreamed he was
walking along the beach with the Lord. Across the sky flashed
scenes from his life. For each scene, he noticed two sets of
footprints in the sand; one belonged to him and the other
to the Lord.*

*When the last scene of his life flashed before him, he
looked back at the footprints in the sand. He noticed that
many times along the path of his life there was only one set
of footprints. He also noticed that it happened at the very
lowest and saddest times in his life. This really bothered
him, and he questioned the Lord about it; "Lord, You
said that once I decided to follow You, You'd walk with
me all the way. But I have noticed that during the most
troublesome times in my life, there was only one set of
footprints, I don't understand why, when I needed You
most, You would leave me."*

*The Lord replied, "My precious, precious child, I love
you and I would never leave you. During your times of
trial and suffering, it was then that I carried you."*

All is Well

Shall I pass through waves of sorrow?
Then I know it will be best
Though I cannot tell the reasons,
I can trust and so am blest.
God is Love and God is faithful,
So in perfect peace I rest.

Say, have you heard that "still small voice"
Above the clamour and the din
Of earth's confusion, Strife and noise,
That softly whispers peace within?

Say, have you heard that "still small voice"
Amidst the heartaches and the fears;
That word in season, sweet and choice,
Which gently dries the rising tears?

The voice which rang o'er Galilee,
When tossed the ship on angry wave,
Still speaks about life's troubled sea,
Still speaks, the weary soul to save.

"Be still and know that I am God,"
Let this the trembling heart rejoice
Admist the fever of unrest
Be still and hear that still small voice.

Deut. 33v27, "Underneath are the everlasting arms". Yes, the everloving arms of our loving Heavenly Father. What a covering is that which our Lord gives to each child or grown-up person He has chosen! For we are chosen even in our mother's womb. Our loving Heavenly Father covers us with His divine presence day and night, not just one day, but He has promised this, His loving presence all our lives. "Please, loving Lord Jesus, make me and help me to be forever conscious of Your abiding presence every moment of every day. Nothing can come to harm us when we are thus covered, for Your banner over us is love.

"Let me lean harder on You, Lord Jesus, nearer and nearer I want to nestle forever close to Your precious wounded side, for there is no safer or surer place, and the peace which You give, even if we are called to a bed of suffering. We thank You, Lord Jesus Christ, our precious Saviour, that the pressure of the pain tells us that You love us very, very dearly.

He Cannot Fail

He cannot fail, for He is God,
He cannot fail, He's pledged His word,
He cannot fail, He will see you through,
'Tis God with whom we have to do.

He cannot fail, He'll send His aid,
He cannot fail, I'm not afraid,
He cannot fail, Oh, praise His Name
The Lord my God is still the same.

Just as He was in days of old,
He loves each sheep within the fold,
He cannot fail – my shepherd true,
He'll lead me on and see me through

And when at last His face I see,
Oh! How I'll praise His love to me,
In His great presence to abide,
Resting – completely satisfied.

When I was ten I had measles very badly, and then
developed an abcess in my right eye. I had to attend Bristol
Royal Eye Infirmary and that year I was given glasses to
wear. Also in the main hospital which was opposite the
Eye Infirmary, Mr. Eyre Brookes said he would do some
operations on my feet. They took two toes off in the end
and later on the chiropodist, Mr. Snell, from Bristol Royal
Infirmary said it would be wise if I had my bunions removed
as well.

This operation was performed by the same surgeon, a
very kind and gracious gentleman. After these operations
were done, the last one being in May in Winford Hospital,
I thanked my surgeon Mr. Eyre Brooke for the tremendous
improvement he had made on my feet and I told him what
my loving Heavenly Father was doing for me through the
wonderful person of God's precious Son, our Lord and
Saviour Jesus Christ.

Mr. Eyre Brooke and his wife wrote back to me, and

said he too, with his family, were walking in the way Jesus would have them walk. I still have the letter for it was such a kind one, and mention was made of Professor Rendle Short who worked in the same hospital and who was such an inspiration to them all.

When I was in the Bristol Royal Infirmary after having the first operation on my feet, being in pain the first night and unable to sleep, a nurse came to ask me if I would like a cup of tea. This Nurse, Hazel Willis, saw my Bible on my locker and we had such a lovely conversation, for she also was a Christian. We made friends, and when I came out of hospital Hazel would often invite me to her home. It was a joy to be able to help Hazel and Douglas get their new home ready before they got married, and two years after I had the joy of nursing and feeding their first baby girl in their home when I was there for the half day.

Now, after three weeks I was back in Müller's Orphanage. Our chief comfort was friendship. We had a strong bond and many keep in touch to this very day of writing this book to the glory of my Lord and Saviour Jesus Christ. He alone has helped me to put pen to paper, and my dear husband David and our dear daughter Christine have encouraged me to write more.

My prayer is that this book may be a great blessing in drawing us all closer to Jesus my precious, precious Saviour who is Lord of my Life. Any reader who has not yet given their hearts to Jesus, I ask of you earnestly to thank Jesus for dying on the Cross of Calvary for you personally, for soon it will be too late, for Jesus is coming back to call all who have thanked Jesus for dying for their sins and who now live for Him. Please *don't* put it off any longer for the time is short!

"For God so loved the world, that He gave His only begotten Son, that whosoever believeth in Him should not perish but have everlasting life" *John 3v16*. Quite a number of people think all their lives that they have to earn their way to Heaven, but this is not so, for Jesus has paid it all. The gospel story in this poem may help someone to trust

Jesus with their lives and thank Him for all He suffered in
the Garden of Gethsemane and on Calvary's Cross.

A Little Pilgrim

One summer's evening ere the sun went down,
When city men were hastening from the town,
To reach their homes, some near at hand, some far,
By snorting train, by omnibus, or car
To be beyond the reach of city's din;
A tram-car stopped, a little girl got in;
A cheerful looking girl, scarce a few years old;
Although not shy her manners were not bold;
But all alone! One scarce could understand,
She held a little bundle in her hand,
A tiny handkerchief with corners tied,
But which did not some bread and butter hide;
A satin scarf, so natty and so neat,
Was o'er her shoulders thrown, she took her seat,
And laid her bundle underneath her arm
And smiling prettily, but yet so calm,
She to the porter said, "May I lie here?"
He answered instantly, "O yes, my dear,"
And there she seemed inclined to make her stay,
While once again the tram went on its way.

The tall conductor, over six feet high,
Now scanned the travellers with a business eye:
But in that eye was something kind and mild,
That took the notice of the little child.
A little after and the man went round,
And soon was heard the old familiar sound,
Of gathering pence, and clipping tickets too,
The tram was full! and he had much to do.
"Your fare, my little girl," at length he said;
She looked a moment, shook her little head;
"I have no pennies; don't you know," said she,
"My fare is paid, and Jesus paid for me?"
He looked, bewildered, and all the people smiled:

60

"I didn't know; and who is Jesus, child?"
"Why, don't you know He once for sinners died,
For little children and for men beside,
To make us good and wash us from our sin;
Is this His railway I am travelling in?"
"Don't think it is! I want your fare you know."
"I told you, Jesus paid it long ago;
My mother told me just before she died,
That Jesus paid when He was crucified;
That at the cross His railway did begin,
Which took poor sinners from a world of sin;
My mother said His home was grand and fair;
I want to go and see my mother there,
I want to go to Heaven, where Jesus lives,
Won't you go too? My mother said He gives
A lovely welcome, shall we not be late?
O let us go before He shuts the gate;
He bids us orphan children come to Him."
The poor conductor's eyes felt rather dim,

He knew not why, he fumbled at his coat,
And felt a lump now rising in his throat,
The people listened to the little child;
Some were in tears, the roughest only smiled
And someone whispered as they looked amazed,
"Out of the mouth of babes the Lord is praised."
"I am a pilgrim," said the little thing;
"I'm going to Heaven, my mother used to sing
To me of Jesus, and His Father's love;
Told me to meet her in His home above,
And so today when a friend went out to tea,
And looking out could not my brother see,
I got my bundle, kissed my little kit,
(I am so hungry, won't you have a bit?)
And got my hat, and then I left my home,
A little pilgrim up to Heaven to roam;
And then your carriage stopped and I could see
You looked so kind, I saw you beckon me,

I thought you must belong to Jesus' train
And are you just going home to Heaven again?"

The poor conductor only shook his head;
Tears in his eyes, the power of speech had fled,
Had conscience by her talking roused his fears,
And struck upon the fountain of his tears;
And made his thoughts in sad confusion whirl?
At last he said. "Once I had a little girl,
I loved her very much; she was my little pet
And with great fondness I remember yet
How much she loved me; but one day she died."
"She's gone to Heaven," the little girl replied;
"She's gone to Jesus – Jesus paid her fare.
Oh, dear conductor, won't you meet her there?"
The poor conductor now broke fairly down;
He could have borne the harshest look or frown,
But no one laughed; but many sitting by
Beheld the scene with sympathetic eye;
He kissed the child, for she his heart had won.
"I am so sleepy," said the little one,
"If you will let me, I'll lay here and wait
Until your carriage comes to Jesus' gate;
Be sure you wake me up and pull my frock,
And at the gate give just one little knock!
And you'll see Jesus there!" The strong man wept!
I could but think as from the carriage I stepped,
How oft a little one has found the road,
The narrow pathway to that blest abode;
Through faith in Christ has read its title clear,
While learned men remain in doubt and fear.
A little child! The Lord oft uses such
To break or bend, the stoutest heart to touch,
Then by His spirit bids the conflict cease,
And once forever enter into peace,
And then along the road the news we bear,
We're going to Heaven because Jesus paid my fare!

We feel that when some great testing or trial comes that we are all alone, but we as orphans were taught that Jesus would be with us all the time, for in God's word He promises that "He will never leave us nor forsake us". *Hebrews 13v5.*

Each day of the month in our bedrooms we were taught to read a chapter from Proverbs. If you are a young person growing up and going through testing times right now, try reading a chapter of Proverbs each day of the month. You will, I can assure you, find great help and such a source of strength. "Trust in the Lord with all your heart; and lean not unto thine own understanding; in all the ways acknowledge Him, and He shall direct thy paths." Proverbs 3v7 goes on, "Be not wise in thine own eyes; fear the Lord and depart from evil." v9: "Honour the Lord with thy substance and with the first fruits of all thine increase." Read on to the end of the book of Proverbs. It was, and still is, such a help to me.

Testimony of an Orphan's Story

Wondrous the Müller story,
Meaning so much to me,
Making my Saviour precious,
To all eternity.
When I was left an orphan,
Without a mother's love,
Müllers a home provided
All praise to God above.

'Twas there we heard of Jesus,
Who left His home above,
To bring us His salvation
And all His wealth of love.
My sin and guilt so pressing
He cleansed away one day,
My heart to Him was opened,
My fears He took away.

'Twas there His word was shown us,
That if we should believe,
We would for life's short journey,
Light, joy and peace receive.
For this so sure foundation,
Laid in those early days,
My song to Thee, Lord Jesus,
Shall radiate Thy praise.

We'll praise for things we knew of,
For shelter, food and care,
Praise too for those things hidden,
The patience, faith and prayer
Of those God called to serve Him,
And labour in His work,
With vision fixed and earnest,
Their task they did not shirk.

So this our Müller story,
We bring to you today,
And give God all the glory,
As we go on our way.
Remembering past mercies
And present blessings too,
Press on to future prospects,
These things I share with you.

I have already mentioned Violet my best friend in the
Orphanage. We would share everything we had given us.
We were great chums! She had a lovely nature, and I well
remember her sister Dorothy had been quite a naughty girl,
and of course she had to be punished, but Violet my friend
looked up in tears to Miss Addis and said, "Please, Miss,
she is my sister, I'll forgive her." With this Violet kissed
her sister Dorothy. What could the teacher do but to forgive
her as well!

Violet was the youngest of a large family. They were left
orphaned when Violet was just a little girl of three. There
were so very many of us orphaned that I would like to write

and tell you of each one and how our Lord Jesus Christ is blessing them, but time will not permit. But I will tell you of a few.

Anne, Joyce and Mary were three sisters. Mary was just a very little girl and she was put playing happily with her toys in her high chair, for they had just finished breakfast. Their mother had wiped the children's hands, and Anne and Joyce were playing happily around their little sister Mary. Mother, bless her, had such a nasty headache, so she put her elbow on the mantle and her hand up to her bad head. It all happened so quickly. The wind caught the mother's skirt and in no time at all she was on fire. Of course the children screamed for they were in the same room.

A neighbour hearing the cries of the children rushed in, saw what had happened and as quick as she could rolled the children's mother in the hearth rug, while another neighbour called for an ambulance. The fire engine came as fast as it could; they soon brought the fire under control but poor Anne, Joyce and Mary's mother died and this is how they came to be at the Orphanage.

Another trio were Kathleen, George and Ken, left orphaned when their mother was giving birth to Ken. Kathleen is now an S.R.N. and a sister in Southmead Hospital. George preaches the wondrous gospel story of saving grace, and Ken sings for his Lord whenever he can. He also sings in a choir. One of the hymns we love to hear him sing is *I Wish I had Given My Saviour More!* and also that lovely hymn *Jesus, the Very Thought of Thee.*

Jesus, the very thought of Thee,
With sweetness fills my breast;
But sweeter far Thy face to see,
And in Thy presence rest.

Jesus our only joy be Thou,
As Thou our prize wilt be;
In Thee be all our glory now,
And through eternity.

Then there was Betty and Violet whose father was in the Navy, but when these girls were very young their mother died of a virus infection. Their Father in the Navy in Plymouth was often away for months out at sea, so he was unable to look after the children when War broke out. When Betty grew up, she did her children's nursing and then married a former orphan, Stan, who was a trained teacher. Both Betty and Violet are very happily married and have lovely children.

Then there is dear aged Miss Grace Norwood, orphaned when quite young and who writes to us regularly. She trusts God, willing to go into the Müller Homes for the elderly this year, a good work which will be a godsend to the elderly.

1986 was the one hundred and fiftieth anniversary of the Müller's Orphanage work, and what can we say as orphans who have been brought up there, but that God has been wonderful and so faithful in caring for our every spiritual need and every physical need as well. We give God all the praise and continually thank Him for all His loving care.

Well do I remember the lovely birthday parties that we had All the children whose birthdays came in the same month had a big family party. It was great! A lovely coloured bow ribbon would be placed around our head and we would sing a song, one of the many that we made up.

All the orphans like a lump of cake,
All the orphans like a lump of cake;
So early in the morning you would hear the teachers
    say,
"All get up and dress yourselves,
There's cake for tea today."

We had put it to a tune, as we did with all the songs we made up. We only had cake for tea on Sundays and tart for tea on Wednesdays, so on birthdays and especially on George Müller's birthday, 27th September, we would rise early in the morning.

By 6.30 a.m. on this special day friends from every

assembly in Bristol, as well as Christians from many parts of England, and some from as far away as Canada and America would come to give praise to our loving Heavenly Father for His continued care of the orphans. Many of these dear people brought gifts of money and other things as thank offerings for their families, but wanted also to give to our needs because God had touched their hearts.

God's love goes on and on and on. He is moving men and women's hearts all the time, all over the world to give to the wonderful work of the Müller's Orphanage. We truly have a great big wonderful God who is always watching over us, supplying our every need!

One older orphan, a boy who went to Müller prayer meetings on many occasions, was heard to pray; "Thank You, loving Heavenly Father, that You saw my great need without parents; You opened those big protecting doors to me. The loving care and Christian teaching I received in Müller's Orphanage I can never forget. Thank You, loving Heavenly Father; the life and work and faith of Mr. George Müller is an abiding influence in my life, for which I humbly thank You, loving Heavenly Father. In Jesus' Name accept my grateful thanks, Amen."

The tears stream down many a face each year, as spontaneous thanks arise for all God's great faithfulness over the years; and He is thanked again and again for all He is going to do for them still.

As recorded in the book about Sister Abigail, Abigail Luff's father was a close friend of George Müller. Early one morning Abigail was playing in Mr. Müller's garden at the orphanage. George Müller, a kindly man, took her by the hand saying, "Come, see what our loving Heavenly Father will do", and he led her into a long dining room. The plates and cups and bowls were on the table.

There was nothing on the table but empty dishes, and no food in the larder to feed all those thousands of orphans and no more money to supply the need. Now what did George Müller do; he called the children in, lifted his hands and eyes in prayer and from his heart thanked God that He would supply food for the children for breakfast before going to school. "Before they call I will answer, and while they are yet speaking I will hear":– A knock at the door was heard; the baker stood there and said, "My wife and I have been unable to sleep."

They both felt that George Müller and his staff were praying because they hadn't any bread, so he got up at two o'clock and baked some fresh bread and said, "I believe the Lord wanted us to send it into you and your orphans."

George Müller thanked the baker and praised God for His care, then said "Children, we have not only bread, but the rare treat of fresh bread." No sooner had he said this than there came a second knock at the door. This time it was a milkman. He announced that his milk cart had broken down right outside the Müller's Orphanage where there were 2,000 orphan children sitting down waiting for God to answer George Müller's prayers to supply their breakfast. The milkman said he would like to give the children his milk churns full of fresh milk, so that he could empty his waggon and repair it. So again George Müller with the children and staff thanked our loving Heavenly Father for sending them food that day.

The greater part of the supply for the orphans came direct from gifts, and as the years went by dedicated servants of God would offer their wages back rather than see the children go short. God always answered their prayers. Sometimes they had to wait, sometimes it was an immediate answer as you have just heard.

Each year we are absolutely thrilled to read the day-to-day account of how God blesses, in gifts of money sent in daily. At harvest time I remember farmers as far as Cornwall coming to the door of No. 3 orphanage with a large lorry full of fruit and vegetables, and also gifts of money. My heart would send up grateful thanks to our loving Heavenly Father for providing for our needs. I would thank them myself, and the Directors would write and thank for every loving gift. These dear farmers and their wives, with kind friends from churches that they met with, would send the gifts of money. Now this did not only happen one year, but every year the same farmers would drive up to Bristol, and Harvest Thank Offerings would come from all over Bristol.

One day I remember well was when I was about twelve and we had taken a walk down to the shops in Gloucester Road. War was over, so our fears were stilled for we knew now that no German planes would be flying over to drop any bombs. How we thanked our loving Heavenly Father for the peace He alone had given to England. Living without parents throughout the War was not easy, for there's nothing more comforting here on earth when you have fears than to be held by your loving parents, but God took great care of us each one, for He loved us all dearly. He had given me that wonderful promise, when just a little girl, "I will not leave you as orphans; I will comfort you" *John 14v18*.

This time we were taking a walk around the shops. It was just before Christmas and my brother Herbert was now eighteen and earning money, so he said in a letter he would be coming to see me at the orphanage on the following Monday, and I was to tell him what I would like for Christmas. I chose a Bible of my very own, and from a shop window in Gloucester Road my brother brought me lovely doll dressed all in pink. I was so delighted with her, I called her Rosemary as it was my favourite name.

On the day before Christmas we were out for a walk, and a butcher came out of his shop with a large box of fifty steak and kidney pies. How it made our mouths water, for we had never tasted a steak and kidney pie before. This was a gift from this kind butcher. He had seen us out for a walk, and his heart was so touched to see so many orphans and he was moved to give us this kind gift. We thanked him ever so much and took them back to the Orphanage, where we thanked our loving Heavenly Father for again providing for our needs. We did so enjoy them for tea that day as they were large pies. They were divided into four, so that two hundred children could have a portion. So that was one of the very many answers of prayer.

CHAPTER EIGHT

Growth and Guidance

In my day in Müller's Orphanage there were three high-lights in the year: George Müller's birthday on 27th September, still remembered with thanksgiving and tea each year; Christmas; and the Purdown Outings.

The outings to Purdown were great fun. They were started off by Mr. Millidge and Mr. Green, then later by Mr. Tilsley or Mr. McCready coming to talk to us all, and praying for safety, a fine day, and most of all for God's wonderful blessing upon us. The staff worked hard to give us such a happy day. We all had a bag of sweets, this in itself was a great treat, a bag of sandwiches and a one pound slice of George Müller's cake. Our eyes almost popped out in excitement!

A van load of ice creams were also brought and each of us had one. In my mind's eye I can see the teachers now. They would have a large tub of cold water and put each ice cream with paper on into cold water. This meant the paper could be taken off easily and none of the ice cream would be left on the paper. It would then be put into a cone and handed out. They went down a real treat on a hot summers outing day!

The day of this outing to Purdown used to thrill not only we orphans, but also all those who lived around the orphanages, for there are literally hundreds of houses and the people would all come out of their front doors to cheer us on our way and wish us a happy day. We in reply would thank them, and hundreds of us used to sing back. We sang a song that we made up. It went like this:

"Mr. Millidge came to tell us
That we are getting ready,
To go for the day

And we are all on our way,
Hip! Hip! Hoorah!
We are off for the day,
To see all the orphans running on the way.
Bless Mr. Tilsley,
Bless Mr. Green,
Bless all the house girls
For making us so clean!

This was just one of many ditties we made up. We also picked blackberries which was great fun each year. Most of our mouths were purple from eating many blackberries, but there were hundreds of us and so we picked very many basins and baskets full which were brought back to the homes to stew, or to make blackberry jelly. I wish the readers of this book could also have heard us, as more than fifteen hundred would sing together in parts; voices ringing out in great enthusiasm and praise to God, as with very thankful hearts we recorded His love and care towards us. It would have thrilled your hearts to have heard so many orphans singing. We had a wonderful choir and I was excited to be in it with many of my friends. We had our special hymn book and I had mine, a gilt edged edition as a prize for swimming in 1948. I was never allowed to dive because of my back, but swimming was good exercise for back trouble.

Now the girls and boys had a high standard of education, reaching Grade 7 and X7. Reading, Writing, English and Arithmetic were the main subjects. Religious Education was really good, for our teachers made the word of God live because it was a living reality in their own hearts.

Some of our teachers were called to the mission field. I remember one teacher especially who when I came out of hospital they were praying for, Miss Mary Bardsley, who went out as a Missionary to India. She did her S.R.N. before going out, so was able to use this gift as well for her Lord in training young Indian ladies to be nurses.

In the Müller reports it is always so interesting to read

answers to the prayers of many missionaries all around the world. It was a great thrill to read how our Lord uses some of these dedicated lives for Himself, and I could tell you of many of them but one will suffice for now: Doctor Stuart Harverson who was a missionary from New Zealand, where he spent his early years of childhood. After several years as a China Inland Mission doctor he went to Nigeria, also Hong Kong, and then moved to South Vietnam where he dedicated his life to the ministry for his Lord in caring for the war orphans in South Vietnam.

The children simply loved him, and during his time there he pointed many orphaned children to our wonderful Saviour who died for them on Calvary's Cross and who rose for them and now lives for them in Heaven and who is one day coming back for them to take them to Heaven. This doctor, through faith in God, built an orphanage. It's wonderful to read of many answers to his prayers. Doctor Harverson took particular interest in a little blind boy called Lip, meaning "poor vision". This boy was taken on a Navy American hospital ship, to see if the surgeon on board the ship called the Repose could give him an operation which would help give him some eyesight back.

He was not able to restore his eyesight, but this blind boy had trusted and thanked Jesus for dying for him, and little Lip was telling others about his wonderful friend Jesus who was never going to leave him nor forsake him.

They all loved Lip, and he would put hymns on a cassette which Doctor Harverson had given him. They could all see that he had something in his life that they had not got. So, dear reader, even if you are crippled, blind, deaf, or orphaned young in years, Jesus wants us to come to Him just as we are. He can, once we have asked Him into our life, use us for His glory in being faithful in witnessing for Him. He will do the rest by His Holy Spirit drawing whom He will to Himself.

Our prayers have followed this blind boy, and other Christian orphans, and Doctor Stuart Harverson. One dear man wrote of Doctor Stuart Harverson, "He is a man who is in love with Christ." Jesus, our precious Saviour, can be your Saviour too. Won't you trust Him with your life before it is too late?

It is interesting to note for the reader's sake, that God is so very faithful in providing for the needs of the orphans in Müllers, but Müllers constantly provide for the need of these missionaries as well as they are led by God. Each boy and girl, on leaving the Orphanage, is given a Bible, the traveller's guide, and other helpful Bible booklets to help them upon life's way. Each of them is counselled to start their day with God by reading His word and talking to Him in prayer. From our early days I was taught the Holy Scriptures with the other children, which were able to make me wise unto salvation through faith which is in Christ Jesus, my Lord. (*2 Timothy 3v15*).

The boys then left at the age of fifteen and were provided with the changes of clothing that they would need. Many friends who were interested prayerfully wrote and asked if they could have a boy or a girl to work for them. So some of the boys would go on farms, some have done their teacher training, and one at least did training to be a doctor. The girls left at seventeen.

Long before I was this age some Christians came to Müller's Homes to see if they could adopt me. Mr. and Mrs. Eggleton had a talk with the Director, and he said to them, "We know you have a lovely Christian home and would love and care for Thelma," but they were told that Mr. Müller found it was not wise to part too soon with any child in his care. He added, "Thelma is not a strong child, and is in the constant care of Doctor Bergin and Sister Duker."

These friends appreciated the talk, and the Director said, "You can have Thelma out for tea to your home whenever you like." This I loved, and they were so kind to me and I have loved their friendship over forty years, and of course my husband David was welcomed to their home. Little Christine was just a baby in arms when she first slept in their home.

74

Many girls, when they leave the care of Müllers, are guided to train as nurses, some as teachers. My best friend trained as a teacher. You will hear later on in the book how my loving Heavenly Father opened up for me to do children's nursing to the Glory of God. He was going to show what He could do through the weak. We give all the praise to our loving Heavenly Father for all His faithfulness in caring and guiding us each one.

"How good is the God we adore,
Our faithful unchangeable friend.
His love is as great as His power,
And knows neither measure nor end."

The girls were able to choose the colour coat, three dresses and hat, shoes, scarf and gloves they would like. Also they were given some money to leave with; such is the great kindness to us from our loving Heavenly Father. We may have been left as orphans, but how much more precious it has been for us to have our loving Heavenly Father to love and care for us so tenderly through all of life's pathway down here.

There is a book written which I have given to many of my friends. It's called "The Best Is Yet To Be." Yes, when we are caught up to be with our precious Jesus, what a day of rejoicing that will be!

Miss Hopper was our head teacher in Müllers, and throughout top school she seemed to like our class, and asked the other teachers if she could keep us all the time, five years in all. We all seemed to learn well under her instruction. I well remember Religious Education with her. She took the life of Hezekiah. The memory has always remained with me.

Miss Hopper spoke of the time when Hezekiah had a letter containing bad news, and spead it before the Lord, and prayed. This lesson was a great help to me as Miss Hopper said so sincerely, "Anything we do not understand in, life, just give your life to Christ and ask Him to show you everything from His precious Word for every situation." God gave a wonderful answer to Hezekiah. You will be able to read about it in *2 Kings 19*.

In the afternoons Miss Hopper took us for knitting and sewing. She told us she had a message from the Bible about knitters, although we are not taught about knitting in the Bible! "Let us see what we can find for our good," she said. "You are familiar with 'casting on'; this means there must always be a beginning. Not much use having the needles and wool in your hands, and even the pattern before you, if you don't cast on! You must always begin by using the things already in your hand."

Then she reminded us that we read in *Exodus 4v2* that the Lord asked Moses, "What is that in thine hand?" Just a rod! But see what use God made of the thing in his hand! "Take a good look," she said, "and see if God has entrusted you with some gift that He wants you to begin using for Him. Casting on stitches, as it were, the very beginning of a piece of work for Him. Or it could even be the knowledge of knitting that could be used to help another who is not so capable in that respect as you are. Cast on one stitch at a time, and soon the needles will carry the increasing weight of your work.

"The thought takes us to that very precious verse in *I Peter 5v7*. One you know so well, but one I would suggest you think about when you are knitting. It won't surprise me if your job becomes one of relaxation when the Lord is in our thoughts. Listen," she said, "to that verse in *I Peter 5v7*. 'Casting all your care upon Him, for He careth for you'; then like the knitting, God has a pattern for your life and God's precious word 'will be a lamp unto our feet and a light unto our path.' *Psalm 119v105*. It is only as we look to Jesus and follow His instructions that the pattern He has planned will be worked out in us."

Dr. Frank Bergin was our doctor at Müllers when I came out of Frenchay Hospital in Bristol. He always took particular care of me at our famous Christmas parties which were enjoyed by all the children and staff, Directors, Doctors, Sisters, Nurses, Teachers, Masters and lots of outside friends. With so many children and staff around the games were fun, but you would always see dear fatherly Dr. Frank Bergin with me and Christine Gale on his knees. We would sit by the Christmas tree lit up with fairy lights and full of gifts for every child. I used to love to feel his strong arms around me.

Christine Gale was a friend of mine. She was two years older than I was, and she used to have to wear callipers on her legs to strengthen them. Dr. M. Packer took over from Dr. Bergin when he was called to Heaven, but more will be told about Dr. Packer in another part of my story.

Dr. Edwards was an outside doctor with his own practice. A very gracious kind man of God. Never will I forget that first Christmas after I had left the hospital as a little girl back in Müller's Orphanage. This kind man bought toys for every single child in the Orphanage. Our eyes almost popped out of our heads when we saw as a gift a large basket of toys. I was given twin baby dolls in a cot with babies' bottles as well; I was absolutely thrilled!

He wasn't there for me to thank him, so when I went to kneel down by my bed that night, I did so much thank Jesus instead for providing us not only with food and clothing, but also for giving us friends and toys and books. I asked God to bless Dr. Edwards for his kindness in giving us toys for Christmas. These labours of love our loving Heavenly Father takes note of, and one day He will reward every kindness done in His Name. The Directors wrote and thanked Dr. Edwards, and the older girls and boys did too.

Professor Rendle Short, a surgeon well known in Bristol and a very godly man, never performed an operation without bending over the patient who was unconscious before him and asking God to guide his hands while performing the operation. God always answered his prayers. He took a keen interest in the orphans, and after the War paid for all of us to go to Bristol Zoo. "Oh, what lovely gardens," we would exclaim with sheer delight, and when we were asked if we would like a ride on Rosie the elephant we were thrilled! I remember how well we were strapped in.

Many gifts like this kind people gave. Many also knitted garments and hand made dresses for us. The same applies still, for the wonderful work goes on for the glory of God. May I at this point say a big Thank You from the bottom of my heart for all your prayers, without which I would never be alive to tell this story for the glory of our wonderful Heavenly Father.

Sister Ellen Petherick was a great friend of Sister Duker. In 1888 Ellen Petherick was taken to Müllers No. 1 orphan house with her sister. Ellen was a wee babe in arms and her very aged grandmother took her up to Bristol. Her grandmother was so delicate and had lost her husband. Ellen's mother and father had died; so the wee babe was placed in the arms of George Müller. When she grew up Ellen did her nursing training in Plymouth, then went back to Müllers and nursed the sick boys and was known as Sister Petherick.

In late 1939 War broke out, and in 1940 the bombs seemed to be falling thick and fast. American soldiers not only came to take over Frenchay Hospital but also had to take over one of the orphan houses. The infants were in No. 5 orphanage, and we shall never forget it. We with many, many older children had to dress up completely with our capes and bonnets on. We then all had to carry a plate, a mug, spoon, knife and fork. This was to help the staff who would have had to carry it all themselves, and it was good to teach us children to be useful. We had to carry everything across the road to No. 3 orphanage where all the Directors and their staff worked. I am reminded that we looked rather like the Children of Israel on that day!

One Sunday night we remember well was when we were now in No. 3 orphanage. It was almost six o'clock and we were all assembled to have our usual Gospel service (hundreds of us remember) when an outside local speaker, Mr. Haynes, came running in to give the warning that enemy planes were just approaching. This meant that bombs would soon be falling. We remember well the staff and children quickly praying for safety. Mr. Haynes told us that night about Peter being released from prison by an angel. They had had all night prayer meetings for him, and God answered their prayers in a wonderful way.

Each Wednesday morning, Mr. C. Smyth would come and give us a message which God had given him from His precious word. The Wednesday after Mr. Haynes had spoken on the Sunday, Mr. Smyth read from the Scriptures. *Psalm 91v7* "A thousand shall fall at thy side, and ten thousand at thy right hand; but it shall not come nigh thee." Afterwards hs spoke on "fear not". True enough God always answered our prayers and kept us safe.

Before Mr. Smyth spoke, a bomb fell on the outside garden wall. Mr. and Mrs. Woods, who lived in the front garden lodge, would remember it well. Our loving Heavenly Father protected us from all harm, such was His great faithfulness. With His protection the blast of the bomb blew the windows in where the children weren't, and where they were all assembled for prayers the windows blew *out*, so not one child was hurt in any way, and not one of the staff was harmed either.

Now, as I say, in 1940 it became very frightening for the little ones, for when the sirens went we had to get out of our beds quickly, put our pillows on our backs, and half asleep we would make our way down the four flights of stairs from our dormitories on the fourth floor. We would then arrive at the basement, where the mattresses had been placed all over the floor and we would have to stay until the "all clear". We little ones had Micky Mouse gas masks.

The staff were wonderful to us, for it was no easy task looking after so many frightened children. They would get us singing all the choruses that we knew, four hundred in all, but one that rang out in those days was,

"God will take care of you all through the day,
He will be with you along life's way."

79

The American soldiers loved hearing so very man[y] orphans singing "God is still on the throne."

The five orphanages were very large and housed over tw[o] thousand orphans. These homes stand on the big hill o[f] Ashley Down, and can still be seen from miles around i[n] Bristol. They are now used as a college.

The War got worse and many hundreds of people los[t] their homes. Whole roads sometimes were destroyed, n[ot] only in Bristol but all around London and other big citie[s] in England. Many died. This also meant that there wer[e] more and more orphans coming in to be cared for by God[.] They cried and cried having lost their mums and dads an[d] whole families during the War.

We infant children were taken to a safer part of Bristo[l] Hampton House, Cotham Park, where the corridor sta[ff] now work, and is now known as Müller House. One nigh[t] I can testify to the wonderful protection upon all we litt[le] ones when God took care of us in Hampton House. Th[at] night a teacher came up to our dormitory to fetch her torc[h] which she had accidently left on the mantlepiece. As sh[e] came up, Miss Joyce smelt smoke; a small incendiary bom[b] had come through the roof, fallen where three empty bed[s] were and left the mattresses smouldering. Had God n[ot] guided her to come up, we would have been in troubl[e.] We were all evacuated during the night. Miss Cornwal[l] Mis Hickford, Miss Forshaw, Miss Scott, Miss Beard, Mi[ss] Kemp, Miss Joyce, Miss Addis and Miss Burrows wer[e] wonderful, so were the masters all dedicated to the wor[k] of caring for the orphans.

During the War we were told that many people who live[d] near to the orphan homes would be crouched down by o[ur] outside front walls when the sirens went, for they sai[d] "We know God is protecting the orphans!"

Now in 1940, on Sunday, 13th October, I was sitting wit[h] Sister Duker alone in the infirmary of No. 3 orphanage. S[he] said, "Come with me, dear, and we will listen to Prince[ss] Elizabeth giving her first broadcast." Her Royal Highne[ss] Princess Elizabeth's message was particularly a very gre[at] comfort to me I well remember, for her message was full of sympathy for all children who were orphans, and also she spoke to children who had to be evacuated, and so were separated from their parents, homes and families.

Her Royal Highness' voice rang out so clearly and said, "My sister Margaret Rose and I feel so much for you, as we know from experience what it means to be away from those we love most of all."

Sister Duker sat me on her knee as tears had come to my eyes. She put a sweet in my mouth to suck to give me comfort as well, and took a book and read me a bedtime story. After that she took off my thick leather spinal jacket and gave me a hot bath. She put a large towel on her knees and lifted me out of the bath to dry me. Putting the spinal jacket back on (as I had to sleep in it for many years) she carried me to my cot and prayed with me, then gave me a cuddle and a kiss goodnight. This individual attention was so very good for me as I did miss my mother and father so very much.

I believe my loving Heavenly Father knew I would need this special individual attention, as I needed so much affection during the War days, as with the great trauma of my parents dying of tuberculosis, and then the four years in hospital with tuberculosis of the spine, and then the War days following on immediately, it was almost too much to bear for one so young. So I believe my loving Heavenly Father gave me the sickness to bear so I could have the individual attention.

As you will recall, there were so many of us orphaned that individual attention was almost impossible, but God did meet my needs. He said "I will not leave you as orphans; I will comfort you." *John 14v18*. How I thank Him for His great love towards me.

"Great was His kindness,
Great was his love,
Sending my Saviour from Heaven above."

England owes such gratitude to God for keeping the

Germans back from setting foot on English soil. Praise to our wonderful God who will always protect His own. The churches and chapels were full during, and just after the War, all having thanksgiving services and thanking God that War was over; but we must never ever forget those who gave their lives in the War and many who are maimed for life. Many lost their eyesight, some of whom I had the privilege of sitting by and giving Braille copies of "Words of Comfort" and "Way of Salvation" at the St. Dunstans Blind Home when I was much older.

The American soldiers asked the Directors after the War if they could give a party for all of the orphan children. This was in 1946. The Directors granted the wish and they spared no expense. They took us in their jeeps to Bristol Zoo and were asked to take great care of us all. Each soldier took a group of about four children, so none would get lost. One soldier alone was asked to look after me as I was so much weaker than the others. I'm not sure if he came from the Red Cross Corps, but this I do remember, that he had glasses on and looked rather like a photograph I have of my father. He was very kind. I remember him carrying me around the places of interest, as he was told I must not walk too far and was not to get over-tired.

We so very much enjoyed this treat out to the Zoo. When we arrived back at the Orphanage there were literally hundreds of balloons decorating the room. Also a fancy hat for each child. By our plates there was an orange, a box of candy sweets and a packet of Polos. They had brought crepe paper fancy table cloths. Also fancy patterned plates which, after use, could be thrown away. We younger children were so thrilled because the word was passed around that we were going to have pink lemonade. The room looked a picture.

There was jelly and ice cream, also cream buns and cakes which were an extra treat for us all. After tea the American soldiers sang to us. There was a good number of them so their voices rang out loud and clear. They really could not do enough for us, and being orphaned their hearts wen out to us. Most of all I think it is true to say that they loved to hear so very many hundreds of orphans singing praises to our loving Heavenly Father for His continued care towards us.

We then sang to them for about an hour, and the wonderful promises from God's word sung to tunes rang out so clearly and sweetly. Yes, their hearts were touched and we saw many a tear being wiped away from their eyes as we sang "Do your tears roll down your face unbidden, Tell it to Jesus, Tell it to Jesus, Are you anxious what shall be tomorrow, Tell it to Jesus alone."

Some of these soldiers did not know 'my Jesus' as their own personal Saviour, so by our bedside each night we would pray for them, that they also might trust in Jesus, then they would have a true Friend and Guide through life's pathway down here.

We thanked them for this lovely party which they gave us, and for the lovely time spent at the Zoo with them. If any of these Americans should ever read this story, may I in deep appreciation thank them again for the wonderful time that they gave us after the War. Also for their care of us throughout the War years. How we praise and thank our precious loving Heavenly Father for His protection upon us in all our years that we have spent on this wonderful earth that He has created. Such beautiful scenery, the mountains, the lakes, the sunsets, the flowers, the trees, all are His handiwork.

Yes, we may have been orphaned young in years, but to have Jesus as one's own personal Saviour is everything. His precious, precious blood that He shed for us at Calvary, His most sacred prayers for us in the Garden of Gethsemane and His wonderful promises given to us from His precious word we can never thank Him enough, but just fall into His ever loving arms of love and ask Him to help us live and shine for Him all our days.

In our teens it was decided by the Directors and their wives, after much prayer, that there was a need for us all in turn to go for a sea-side holiday, so a holiday home was bought at Minehead. These dedicated Christians would put flowers in our bedrooms. There were about six of us to every room. Oh it was lovely, and to breathe that sea air into our lungs was so very healthy. How we praised and thanked our loving Heavenly Father again and again.

The C.S.S.M. childrens meetings on the beach with Uncle Tom were so good. Also those Sunday school classes by Mr. Mockeridge at the Assembly in Minehead were an extra help in life's pathway. The picnics every day and the walks to Porlock Weir with Mr. and Mrs. McCready, Miss Green and Miss Carp, were so much appreciated and so homely. Then, too was the gathering for morning prayer in Mrs. Green's and Miss Green's sitting room. Miss Green would sometimes sing that piece of music called "Jerusalem". I must say it was sung really beautifully, but when she reached the high notes their pet dog who was with us used to howl his high note too, to the amusement of all!

When we reached the age of fifteen we had to do some training. I said that I would dearly love to be trained as children's nurse and do the N.N.E.B. two year training, but they all said I would not be strong enough. So I had the privilege of looking after all the Directors and their wives, caring for their every need. In the winter, if the snow was falling thick and fast, then it would be my responsibility to ask them if they would like to stay for a while. If they did stay then it would be my responsibility to get a bedroom ready for them, and then provide all their meals for them. It was a delight for me to do tasty dishes for the Directors which they appreciated so much.

In the mornings, when I used to take their breakfast into their room, often it would be the time that Mr. and Mrs. McCready were having their family worship together. Then the rest of the duties throughout the day would be to provide for the needs of the corridor staff as they arrived for duty at ten o'clock. It was not long before they were drinking a cup of tea at eleven o'clock, with one of my home made cakes. Mr. J. Rose tells the story how, when he came for an interview, his fears went when the big door opened and he found the smiling face of Thelma welcoming him in. Mr. Rose was being interviewed in connection with his being the next Director. He took up this post in 1953 and is still the Director in the year I write this book, 1986.

These dear people who loved God, really cared for us. Now, since those early days, the home of Mr. and Mrs. Rouse was opened for me to spend weekends with them. When their youngest daughter Christine was very young I would love to babysit for her. I was invited to tea in many kind people's homes, Mr. and Mrs. Eggleton's home being open to me any time, and many enjoyable weekends and holidays I spent with them. Then dear Mr. and Mrs. Varney's home for tea, Mr. and Mrs. Mason's and Mr. and Mrs. English's home too. Mrs. English was our Bible Class teacher and she was a dear. Also Mr. and Mrs. Nute's home for tea when they first got married.

When I was seventeen I was baptised with many others. Eleven of us were baptised, and Dr. Maurice Packer's daughter Glennis was also baptised on that same night in July 1951. Dr. Maurice Packer took the meeting. There were about three hundred who attended. It was a most moving meeting. On the Sunday after we had been baptised we were at Ebenezer Gospel Hall, Filton Avenue, Bristol where a lovely Evangelist welcomed us in to full fellowship, Mr. Lester Wilson from the U.S.A.

I shall never ever forget Dr. Packer and his dear wife and children. They would invite Irene and me into their home to tea. They were such godly elders in caring for our needs. We would have Christmas parties with them as well and all the Assembly would be invited. They would never have us worry about anything.

At this point I would like to say that Dr. Frank Bergin had been called to Heaven and Dr. Maurice Packer was the doctor for Müller's Orphanage, along with Dr. Alders. One day he signed for me to have another operation on my feet, this time I had to go to the country hospital at Winford, just south of Bristol. The Sister was a dear, and knowing I was very happy there, she asked if she could keep me in hospital for another week. My bed along with others was placed right in front of the french windows, where we could see the primroses around the trees and each day a farmer's cow would pass by at the same time.

I was in for the removal of bunions, and I made some really lovely friends. One was Mrs. Hilda Harman who had T.B. spine. When I could get out of bed she and others asked me to go to their beds and tell them why I was so happy. So I told them that it was really Jesus shining out of my heart, and we talked for a long time. I gave them the book "Peace with God" written by Billy Graham which had been a great help to me, also the life of George Müller telling how he with God's help looked after so many thousands of orphans, *and I was one of them*!

They listened with great interest to the story of what my loving Heavenly Father had done for me. Hilda trusted Jesus as her own personal Saviour. Three weeks after that, Hilda was called to Heaven. Joan, in the next bed to her, had her Bible brought in to her. She said she wanted "to lead a different life from now."

I just loved the singing that we had on Sundays in that hospital with the hospital's Minister. The young girl in the bed by me was only twelve, and loved to pull a promise out of my promise box. The lady in the bed the other side of me had back trouble and had a disc removed. She came back to Jesus and told her husband that when she came out of the hospital their life style was going to change in their family. "All for the good," she said.

When I came out of hospital I was due to see Dr. Maurice Packer to make sure my feet were giving no trouble. He and his wife, and his brother, Mr. Ronald Packer who was on the staff of Müllers, were very kind and Dr. Packer asked what I wanted to do for God in my life. I told him I had prayed such a lot about the matter and I felt God would have me do my children's nursing. He asked me what was holding me back now that my operations were finished. I opened up and explained that I was repeatedly told that I would not be strong enough. So that week he and his wife asked me around to their home for tea and to pray about doing my training. The talk was such a help, like a daughter or son would get from loving parents. God had done so much and He had promised He would show me His will for my life.

The next week Miss McClements went to be with her Lord in Heaven. She was such a lovely kind lady whom we were all fond of. Mrs. Peggy Scroggie, her sister, wrote and asked me if I would like to leave Müllers and live with her and her husband, Mr. James Scroggie, and look after her eight year old son David. Mrs. Scroggie was doing Health Visitors training. When I wrote back I said I would love to go and live with them in Hove, Sussex, as long as I could do my children's nursing training.

She replied that she had a friend who was the Matron of the Hove Day Nursery. The months went quickly by and after three months I wrote to the Matron who in turn had me examined by the Medical Officer of Hove. He said, "Thelma is not strong enough, having her family die of T.B. and she has had four years in Frenchay Hospital with T.B. spine. It is unwise."

I went on praying about it, then wrote to the Brighton General Hospital. The lecturers were lovely people, and I knew they were fond of me, and they allowed me to do my six weeks training in their school with forty other nurses. One of these lecturers was a married lady, and we were discussing sick children that day, and to my surprise she said, right in front of all the nurses, that there was one nurse she would trust her children to be looked after if they were sick and she called my name. Why, I do not know, for I was one of a number, but I knew that both these nursing sisters showed they were fond of me.

Now not being strong enough to go on the wards, they were ever so sorry to say goodbye and did not want me to go. One of them was a Christian, and she said she and her family would be praying for me and wished me God's blessing. I told her I would write to the Matron of Hove Day Nursery if she could give me a reference to enclose with my letter. I wrote and believed that if I worked there in Hove Day Nursery that I would do my best and show them what God could do through a weak child of His. I worked there nursing the children for nine months, then this time the Matron of Hove Day Nursery wrote a letter to Hove's Medical Officer. I wrote one as well saying I had worked nine months now and Matron had given me a good report.

The Medical Officer of Hove got his married lady doctor to examine me, and she asked me a lot of questions, as to why I wanted to do my training so badly. I explained that I was very fond of children, particularly sick and physically handicapped children, "Because," I said, "I was orphaned at eighteen months through my parents and whole family dying of T.B. Then I was put into a T.B. cot at two years of age because I had it in the spine, so," I said, "to cut a long story short, I feel God will help me to have more understanding for sick children than most, as He has allowed me to suffer."

The lady doctor was so kind and so symapthetic that she got me measured that week for another spinal jacket and guided me how to lift and how not to lift, and told me to lift little babes or toddlers by crouching first. So with their kindness in letting me have the chance to do my children's nursing, a two year training, my loving Heavenly Father guided me and helped me through. The badge and certificate was presented to me at the end of the two year training. Our lecturers were most kind people as well, Miss English and Miss MacKey were real dears and had a love for us all.

CHAPTER NINE

Suffering's Purpose Unfolds

When I had finished my two years children's training at Hove Nursery Training College, we were sent our badge and certificate. Mr. and Mrs. James Scroggie had now moved out of their rented home and bought a small bungalow. David their eleven year old son went to St. Aubyns school in Devon. He was eight when I first came to look after him, as Mrs. Scroggie was doing her Health Visitors training.

The bungalow was small, so Mr. and Mrs. Gander opened up their home to me, their children having all grown up. As I was still going to be in Hove for a while, Mrs. Gander and I would go along to worship at Hove Gospel Hall, Rutland Hall. What lovely saints of God went there. Mr. and Mrs. Scroggie, Mr. and Mrs. Snaith, Mr. and Mrs. Page, Mr. and Mrs. Francis and family, Mr. and Mrs. David Wright, Mr. and Mrs. Miller, Mr. and Mrs. Bridle, the Miss Harris and Miss Sussex and friend, also a blind friend and many more, all of whom opened their homes to me and showed such Christian love and grace. How I thank them all for such kindness. Mr. and Mrs. Gander treated me just as if I was their own daughter.

It was not long after my two years that I felt God calling me to nurse at Chailey Heritage Hospital. I started on November 1st, 1958, and then had such happy times of fellowship at Haywards Heath Gospel Hall, and still today many are coming to Christ and numbers are being added. All of them were such kind and considerate Christians and many a happy time I spent in fellowship with every one of them, also in their homes before a ministry or prayer meeting. How I thank God for every one of them!

Haywards Heath is seven miles from Chailey Heritage Hospital. Many times a young couple with their wee child would come and pick me up, which was so kind of them as the hopsital was seven miles away. Their lovely reply was always, "We are doing this for Jesus, and we welcome you in our home."

Sometimes I would catch the bus into Haywards Heath, and Mrs. Carey and Jean always had a cup of tea and home made fruit cake ready as soon as I got off the bus. Dear aged Mr. and Mrs. Bannister, Mr. and Mrs. Turner, Vi and Basil and Mr. and Mrs. Schooling, all had their homes open for me to come at any time. There was Amy and Dorothy also, and Mrs. Abbott and John and so very many more. It really is wonderful being in the great family of God. Wherever you are in the world, one feels that oneness as soon as you meet.

When I had time off, I would catch the bus back to Hove, one hour's journey from the hospital, and such happy times I spent with Mrs. Gander. Mr. Gander was often at work, but in his spare time grew such delicious vegetables and fruit. The Ganders were so kind in sharing their fruit and vegetables with the elderly and sick, and I would have the pleasure of visiting these dear friends.

Chailey Heritage Hospital began in 1903 when Grace Kimmins came with seven crippled London boys to a large house to give them the benefit of life in the country and a craft training to enable them to earn a living later on. Their funds were a £5 note and the accounts were kept in a penny notebook. But friends gave money to help care for these crippled children, and hearty thanks were given to all who sent in money or clothes. From these beginnings grew Chailey Heritage Hospital which today cares for over two hundred children.

The hospital was taken over by the Ministry of Health under the National Health Service Act in 1948. It is in the heart of Sussex. It is for long-stay physically handicapped children, caring for children whose ages range from a few weeks to sixteen years, and teachers and hospital staff work side by side for the special needs of the physically handicapped child.

The Chailey Heritage has three main sites scattered over 1½ miles of Chailey Common. At the new Heritage Hospital there are six hospital wards (an admission and assessment ward, babies, nursery, junior mixed, senior girls and senior boys wards). There are Physiotherapy, speech and occupational therapy departments, operating theatres, an experimental workshop, an indoor heated swimming pool and a unit for deaf children. Dr. E. P. Quibell has been medical administrator at the Chailey Heritage Hospital since 1950. Dr. Strodes works alongside him. Matron Barnard with Matron McDowell were the matrons when I nursed there so happily. I was on Queen Elizabeth Ward and worked with other trained nurses alongside Sister May. Such a happy ward it was, and all nursing staff and teachers worked so happily as we nursed the children. How I got in to children's nursing having had T.B. spine and still wearing a spinal support to strengthen my spine when lifting, is a story that proves again God's faithfulness to one so weak.

When I had finished my training and qualified, I did so want to witness faithfully for my wonderful Lord who had done so much for me. But despite praying much about it I knew within my heart that I would never pass a medical to be able to go out to be a missionary abroad, so I prayed my Lord would show me which hospital He would have me nurse children and witness for the Glory of God.

Shining

Are you shining for Jesus, dear one?
You have given your heart to Him;
But is the light strong within it,
Or is it but pale and dim?
Can everybody see it,
That Jesus is all to you?
That your love to Him is burning
With radiance warm and true?
Is the seal upon your forehead,
So that it must be known

That you are 'all for Jesus'.
That your heart is all His own?

One day Matron Walters of the Hove Day Nursery called me to see her and said, "The Matron of the Chailey Heritage Hospital was passing through a few days ago and called on me to ask if I had any trained N.N.E.B. children's nurses who would be interested in nursing Chailey's children; just light duties on the toddler ward helping to nurse and care for the thirty-six disabled children they have. They have two hundred children of all ages, so you will see they have many wards. There is also a school for those able to cope with walking and dressing themselves. But Matron Barnard told me it is a very caring type of nurse that they need for this ward. A few are orphans as well as disabled, many are so very ill that they need such a very sympathetic heart to love and care for them.

"I told her I have just the nurse. I said, 'Nurse Thelma Cheeseman has been through so much in her life, and she was orphaned when not even two years of age. She also contracted T.B. from her parents so she lay in a plaster-of-paris cot for four and a half years in Frenchay Hospital, Bristol. After a big spinal operation she had to learn to walk again when she was five. The whole story speaks of God's faithfulness in caring for her. I'm sure she is the one for your need in your hospital.' Matron Barnard said, 'Oh, thank you,' as we finished a cup of tea together. 'I would be ever so grateful if you could ask Nurse Cheeseman when she comes into work tomorrow if she could come for an interview at Chailey Heritage Hospital as soon as possible. She sounds just the nurse for the task.' 'I'll talk to her', I said, 'and get her to go for an interview with you and see around the hospital. I do not really want her to leave this nursery, but she told me the other day that she was praying for a nursing post to open up for her in a hospital, so I'm sure she is the right one for the job.' "

The nurse who was there in the toddler ward at Chailey Hospital was leaving to get married. They had difficulty in replacing her. "Not many girls are anxious to undertake that kind of work and it's such a worthwhile job," Matron Walters went on to say to me. "You've known what it is like to be orphaned, and you would have a special under-standing of these little ones and they want someone to live in, so your accommodation would be solved and on your off duty, one and a half days each week, I know you have many Christian homes opened to you. You will also make new friends from the Haywards Heath Assembly."

I was so full of joy knowing my loving Heavenly Father was guiding and showing me His will as to the type of children to nurse. I went for the interview, and Matron Barnard welcomed me and shook my hand. "When you have had a holiday, what date could you start?" Matron asked. I told her I was to be bridesmaid for my best friend in Bristol, but I could start on November 1st. It was now 1958.

It was a very wet day when Mr. James Scroggie was due to take the gospel service at the Gospel Hall in Haywards Heath at 6.30 p.m. We were invited to tea with dear aged Mr. and Mrs. Bannister, and afterwards Mr. Scroggie drove me to the Chailey Heritage Hospital, which was seven miles away from Haywards Heath. Now of course children have their problems too, and it's not just learning how to cope with their disabilities. It's how to accept the fact that some will never be able to lead normal lives, get married, or have children. Watching other children playing ball and swimming one child looked at the ward sister and asked, "Will I ever be able to do that?" The ward sister on one ward told us, "I try to answer as best I can. I can never say to them 'You'll *never* be able to do it.' After all," she said, "who am I to say that! Even some specialists have been proved wrong."

I have found in my life, having suffered with a tubercu-losis spine for many years, that God has a purpose in all things and He through us can do the impossible if we will thank His Son for dying for us on the cross of Calvary and then give Him our whole lives, our will and all. Just whenever we need to, and just wherever we are, we can speak to Him in prayer and He is always ready to listen to what we have to ask Him. He has promised to supply all our needs, and I have proved God answers prayer.

The reason for telling this story is to help those who may be going through similar trials. I also want to say that Jesus has promised that He "will never leave us nor forsake us".

I believe that when sickness and trials come it is an opportunity usually when people get time to think, and as I look back over my life I can trace the hand of God; why He allowed my parents to be taken at such an early age, and also the reason for suffering in a T.B. cot. The reason was to tell me that He cared and He loves and knows all about everybody in the whole wide world. Throughout my life He has never failed me and He never will; and through all the testings or sickness that may come our way, it is to tell us that He wants to draw us closer to Himself. He is making us His own for etenity.

I really believed God had called me to Chailey Heritage Hospital, and it was such a great privilege to be able to nurse these toddlers and young children. At night time after my nursing was finished for the evening it used to delight my heart, for these little children would put their chubby hands together and say to me, "Nurse Cheesey, prayers please". And around each bed they would love me to tell them a Bible story and pray with each one of them. God's word says, "They shall be Mine, saith the Lord, in that day when I make up My jewels".

Red and yellow, black and white,
Arms and legs are not quite right,
Little bodies racked with pain,
Their little hearts are golden grain.

Their blessings on this earth not great,
But angels white upon them wait,
And like a perfect little dove,
Nurse Thelma coo's sweet words of love.

Their life upon this earth oft short,
To help themselves they must be taught,
But music sweet they do enjoy,
As Thelma says, "He's a lovely boy."

A. T. Bannister

The Matron of Chailey Heritage Hospital had a missionary sister living in India. Matron Barnard and Matron McDowell had a prize-giving afternoon where a few of us nurses had a book presented to us. I was so thrilled to have a book presented to me on the missionary life of Albert Schweitzer. In it was put this lovely prayer for me. I was so touched and thankful.

A Nurse's Prayer

Because the day that stretches out for me
Is full of busy hours, I come to Thee
To ask thee, Lord, that Thou wilt see me through
The many things that I may have to do.
Help me to make my beds the smoothest way;
Help me to make more tempting every tray;
Help me to sense when pain must have relief;
Help me to deal with those borne down by grief.

Help me to take to every patient's room,
The light of life to brighten up the gloom.
Help me to bring to every soul in fear
The sure and steadfast thought that Thou art near.
And if today, or if tonight, maybe,
Some patients in my care set out to sea,
To face the great adventure we call death,
Sustain them, Father, in their parting breath.

Help me to live throughout this live-long day,
As one who loves Thee well, dear Lord, I pray;
And when the day is done and evening stars
Shine through the dark above the sunset bars,
When weary quite, I turn to seek my rest,
Lord, may I truly know I've done my best.

A missionary friend of our came round our ward and we
had a dear West African boy on the ward. He could get
dressed and so was able to move about freely. He tugged
at the missionary's coat and repeated the poem,

"What Colour Was Jesus?"

"What colour was Jesus?" the little lad asked,
As he stood by the missionary's knee,
"Was his skin white like yours,
As your own little boy,
or brown like my brother's, and me?"

The missionary wrinkled his forehead in thought,
and wondered just where to begin.
He pictured the Lord
As a small Jewish boy,
with his beautiful deep olive skin.

"He was darker than me, but lighter than you,"
He explained and then paused in surprise.
For the little face beamed
And the small white Teeth gleamed,
And the happiness shone in his eyes.

"If He's partly like me and partly like you,
He belongs to us all then," he said,
The missionary gazed
At the child all amazed
At the truth that had entered his head.

He belongs to us all, and we all need to know,
What that little West African knew,
He had died for our sin
And whatever our skin,
He's longing to make us anew.

The children who are well enough to get up are washed
and dressed, and sit up at the table provided for them in
the middle of the ward. If it is fine the children are out of
doors all day for schooling and also for meals. It was a little

bit amusing, for while I was helping Christopher to feed himself, another child, Freddie by name, was in a wheelchair being fed by one of the nurses. Now Nurse Hills was really praising Freddie for eating his lunch so well, but little did she know that Freddie had some sparrow friends perched the other side of his wheelchair, and many were on the ground just waiting for him to pass on some of his lunch which they were really enjoying and chirping "Thank you very much"!

As it is not wise for the children to have pets in hospitals, the birds became real friends to the children. The hospital is situated in the heart of the country, and those well enough could be taken for a short walk around the hospital grounds. Often we would find a bird's nest in one of the bushes in the hospital grounds and on one occasion the foresters had been felling trees. It was well after the young had flown from the nest that an empty nest was found. The children found it so interesting and they started to pull it apart to see what it was made of. Pressed down in the nest was a little piece of paper that the parent birds when making their nest had found and picked up. A tiny bit of paper. Guess what was on it! That precious text from *1 Peter 5v7* "Casting all your care upon Him for He careth for you."

Just the end part of the text was in the nest "He careth for you". It was so true, I have never in all my life seen such fat sparrows as were around Chailey Heritage Hospital and especially around Queen Elizabeths Ward for they did so enjoy Freddie's tit bits! And of course Freddie wasn't the only one who put food down for them. No wonder they got so fat. When we got back to the ward one day from our nature walk one child said excitedly to Miss Parker, "The nurses have taught me to pick flowers with my toes." She was born with no arms.

We had little time to spend before giving the children their tea. So, telling the story to Mrs. Parker, the teacher of Q.E.B. Ward, about the nest, and showing it to her with the text, she asked me if I knew a poem about birds. So I taught the older children this one. In fact we learnt it by

singing it to the tune What a Friend We Have in Jesus.
The poem of the birds goes well to that tune!

Said the Robin to the Sparrow,
'I should really like to know,
Why these anxious human beings,
Rush about and worry so."
Said the Sparrow to the Robin,
"Friend, I think that it must be
That they have no Heavenly Father
Such as cares for you and me."

So the Robin and the Sparrow,
Sang their chorus, O how sweet;
"Don't you know that Jesus loves you,
Come and gather round His feet,
He who fed the robin redbreast;
He who marks the sparrow's fall;
He's the Lord who died to save you;
Come and trust Him one and all."

Mrs. Parker had already taught them another one, which
they sang while another nurse and I washed their hands
before tea.

God made little robin
In the days of spring,
"Please," said little robin,
"When am I to sing?
When am I to sing?"

God then spoke to robin,
"You must sing always,
But your sweetest carol,
Keep for wintry days
Keep for wintry days."

Sister May had come on duty by now and the children
were asked to sing, "Thank You for the world so sweet,
Thank You for the food we eat, Thank You for the birds
that sing, Thank You, God, for everything. Amen."

They had homemade fish cakes for their tea that day. The cook in the hospital was excellent, and she had a good staff who worked with her. Phoebe was one of them and they cooked some really delicious meals. It's true to say the children were well cared for in every way. The nursing staff were well catered for, and those delicious meals made us work well. How we thank our loving Heavenly Father for all His love and care.

There are always lots of toys in a children's hospital which kind friends have brought in in appreciation for looking after their children. There are plenty of books for the older ones to read, and picture books for the little ones. There is a dolls' house and a train set that comes out for special occasions and many other toys, plus a record player, for the children just love music. Most of them have somebody in their family to visit them, for all of these have come into hospital from quite a long way from their home.

This is a story of little Mary-Anne, a sweet girl and well loved by all the nursing staff, but one sad thing about Mary is that for all the four and a half years that I was in the hospital I never saw her mother come in to visit her. She was born in Ireland. Mary-Ann was born with a spina-bifida in the middle of her back in the form of a large lump, sometimes the size of a grapefruit which continually weeps; so great care had to be taken that it is well protected with a dressing and a special cap made to fit over it. Mary-Ann was quite a wee baby when she came to the hospital to be nursed and everybody loved her, as they did all the children.

The children wore loose clothing, open vests, often knitted by friends, and smock dresses so that they hung loosely, thus hiding the spina-bifida lump on the back. One dear child with lovely parents had two of these bifidas, one on her back and a large one on her neck. When little Stephen was called to be with Jesus in Heaven I was asked by Sister May to go and be with him at his last moments on earth. He looked like a little angel with his fair curly hair and his white nightdress I put on, and his little hands which were just like wings for he did not have any arms.

When he died, Sister May asked me to carry him out of the side ward up to the church. I wept. He looked so very beautiful, and I felt my loving Heavenly Father's arm all around me as I carried him up to the church which was about fifty yards away. A sacred moment I shall never forget.

I did, and do, thank my loving Heavenly Father for having had the privilege of teaching them the song, "Jesus loves me, this I know, for the Bible tells me so. Little ones to Him belong, we are weak but He is strong." We talked about Jesus often, for He was such a close friend to the children and me.

Mary-Ann, bless her, asked one of the nurses to call me one day to go and sit with her in the side ward for she lay ever so ill. She asked me to sing with her, and she sang out with all the strength that she could muster. "Jesus loves me, loves me still, though I'm very weak and ill. From His shining throne on high, comes to watch me where I lie." She then said to me, "Mummy Cheesey, please carry me to be with Jesus." I realised then that soon, and very soon, the sun was going to set upon her earthly life.

I sat and held her hand, and she kissed my hand as I held a glass of fresh water for her to sip. They were all so beautiful, those whom God was calling to sing among his angels. Little Christopher also and little Wendy; I had the privilege of bathing these two in their cots every day, for they needed special care. They also went to sing among the angels for they loved Jesus very much. Yes, we do weep with those who weep. Dear Grandma Coleman and Wendy's father loved her dearly, but they could accept that it was far better for Wendy to go to Heaven, as she would never be better. She was so very ill and was getting weaker each month. She could not speak the last few months, but she had a lovely smile and would smile up at me as I sang to her of the love of Jesus. Wendy was five and so was Mary-Ann. Christopher was four and Stephen was two when Jesus took them safely home to Heaven. Alex also went, when he was ten.

> Safe in the arms of Jesus,
> Safe on His gentle breast,
> There by His love o'er-shaded,
> Sweetly my soul shall rest.
> Harts 'tis the voice of angels,
> Borne in a song to me
> Over the fields of glory,
> Over the Jasper Sea.

Only seven though, out of two hundred, were called to Heaven. In an Orthopaedic Hospital the children usually get stronger and are able to go home once they have learnt to walk and dress themselves. In August a new holiday home for the Chailey children was opened in Hove, Sussex. It was a large house that was given to the hospital by Mary Fuller of Cowden. In August 1963 the first group of eight children moved in. What lovely times they had. They also enjoyed the barbecues on the beach. Passers-by always stopped to talk to the children, and many dropped in for a chat or to lend a hand. Yes, despite the deformities they were given such a happy time in hospital and in the holiday homes. Philip came as far as Bideford for a holiday and we were able to have him for a day in our home when we were married.

CHAPTER TEN

A Home Together

It was towards the end of my four and a half years nursing at Chailey Heritage Hospital that I met David. I had been praying often that if it was the Lord's will for me, He would lead the partner of His choice to me. I was also praying that the partner would be one of God's children who would be used by the Lord to study His word and tell others about Him.

Prayer also rose to the throne of grace, knowing our precious Heavenly Father has promised to supply all our needs concerning a home where we could live together for His glory. We met at a holiday centre in Eastbourne in 1960. There were 180 Christians gathered together at a Bible Conference at Victoria Park Hotel. Friends of all ages had come from as far away as Scotland, Wales, Sussex, Devon and Cornwall. In the afternoon we all made friends, and if there was anybody on their own it was not long before others had welcomed them to join in any car trips or coach trips, so in this way there were no lonely ones.

We visited the Alfriston Butterfly Farm which was certainly a very beautiful place. To move from the study of God's word, to observing God's wonderful creation was a sheer delight to all who like the beauty of our loving Heavenly Father's handiwork in scenes of creation. We would also admire the beauty of the Sussex Downs. Beachy Head was one favourite place of ours in Sussex. On Sundays we shared a very precious morning worship meeting, worshipping our precious Lord and Saviour Jesus Christ. The theme of that worship meeting was taken from the first hymn given out, guided by The Holy Spirit.

Majestic Sweetness Sits Enthroned

Majestic sweetness sits enthroned
Upon the Saviour's brow;
His head with radiant glories crowned,
His lips with grace o'erflow.

No mortal can with Him compare,
Among the sons of men;
Fairer is He than all the fair,
That fill the Heavenly train.

He saw me plunged in deep distress,
He flew to my relief,
For me He bore the shameful cross
And carried all my grief.

To Him I owe my life and breath,
And all the joys I have;
He makes me triumph over death,
He saves me from the grave.

To Heaven, the place of His abode,
He brings my weary feet;
Shows me the glories of my God,
And makes my joy complete.

Since from His bounty I receive,
Such proofs of love divine,
Had I a thousand hearts to give,
Lord, they should all be Thine!

Jesus in His precious word had His disciples gathered together in the Uppr Room, just before the cross, "to call Himself to mind" by partaking of bread and wine. "Do this," He said, "in remembrance of Me. This bread is a symbol of My precious body which is given for you. The wine a symbol of My precious blood shed for you. I want all My believers who have been forgiven of their sins to keep this feast, showing my death until I come."

Jesus said to His disciples in John 14v15 before He went

back to Heaven, "If ye love Me, keep My commandments, and I will pray the Father and He shall give you another "Comforter", that He may abide with you for ever; (v17) even the Spirit of truth; whom the world cannot receive because it seeth Him not, neither knoweth Him; but ye know Him; for He dwelleth with you and shall be in you."

We walked back to the hotel from the worship service. The sun was shining, the birds were singing praise to their Heavenly Creator; it really was a lovely walk as we talked and pondered on the morning's worship of our precious Saviour Jesus Christ.

> Living He loved me, dying He saved me,
> Buried He carried my sins far away,
> Rising He justified freely forever,
> One day He's coming, oh glorious day!

We sang this as we walked along. In the morning gathering we were reminded of His sweet and precious face and one breathed, "Oh, make me meet to follow the steps of Thy wounded feet." Our thoughts were now for the souls of men. "I have lost my life to find it again, e're since one day in a quiet place, I met my Master face to face." Yes, it was a truly precious walk back to the hotel. We were ever so conscious of our Lord's presence.

At the hotel our mid-day lunch was ready. We were all encouraged to sit around at small tables and move to different tables each day, therefore allowing us to meet new friends. It was on Friday morning that David came and sat at the table where I was. David started talking to me and he asked me where I was born, so I told him it was in Wembury, Devon, five miles from Plymouth. Then he asked me what my father did and I said that he was in the Navy, based at Plymouth, before he and my mother died of tuberculosis. "I have spent years in hospital with T.B. of the spine," I told him.

I noticed David listening with an expression that suggested special sympathy. "That really is amazing," he said eventually. "My father was in the Navy based at

104

Plymouth too, and I spent most of my teenage years suffering from T.B. of the lung and hip. We certainly have a lot in common!"

As soon as the morning conference was over we found a quiet spot in the lounge where we talked for a long time, while we shared our stories. Punctuated by a few leading questions, I tumbled out the history of early family days with Mary-Flora and Herbert, and the great heartbreak of losing both parents and my years in Frenchay Hospital and Müller's Orphanage.

David in turn told me that he lived at a grocery shop in Devon, which had been in the family for years and years. He went on to explain that his father had been killed in the early months of the War, when his ship H.M.S. Fame was bombed. He was only two years old, and his brother Royston ten when their father died. His mother had returned with her two sons to the family home and shop, owned and run by her unmarried sister, Aunt Maud. David looked at me. "How old were you and your brother and sister when your parents died"?

"My brother Herbert was only eight, my sister Mary-Flora seven and myself just eighteen months old," I said quickly.

"That's very, very sad," I remember David saying with feeling.

I looked up to David and said, "Jesus my precious Saviour has been my best friend all through my life. Without His keeping power I could never have survived. The way He has graciously answered prayer is just so wonderful."

Later that day David asked me out for a quiet stroll. "Where are you living now? And where do you work?" were his questions. Gladly I described my call to nurse the children of Chailey Heritage Hospital.

"The hospital lies in the heart of Sussex, and the country-side is so beautiful around," I told him. "I find the work so very rewarding! Some of the little children have no arms or legs. Those without arms, we teach them to feed themselves by placing a low tray on a stand before them. We then place a spoon in between their toes and with patience, help to guide their foot up to their mouth. We have to teach them this skill very young."

By now we were back at our hotel, and seeing David's interest I ran quickly to my room. A few minutes later I rejoined him, holding a copy of the Scripture Gift Mission's Magazine of the Young Sowers League. A year earlier I had written to Y.S.L. asking permission for their Bible searching scheme to be adapted to the needs of a few children unable to use their hands. This they gladly supplied, and the magazine I held showed a photograph of Rosemary who with my help had completed the New Testaement course, writing every reference with a pen held in her mouth.

In response to David's obvious interest I promised to introduce him to the children one day, a promise I was certainly going to have to keep, as David said he would dearly love to meet them. The next day we all had to leave but not before we promised to continue our friendship by writing to each other and so began the story which led, on 24th February 1963, to our engagement. We still have the letters we wrote to each other in a box tied now with red ribbon. We looked forward so much to our letters and regular 'phone calls. We always made sure we were at the 'phone in plenty of time. David's rich deep voice used to give me a thrill and the nurses said I would go quite pink!

Though two hundred miles apart we managed to meet for a weekend in Kent and then, at Christmas, even though I was on duty Christmas Day, I had sufficient leave to travel to Devon and meet David's family. We had already sent each other our Christmas gifts. Mine to David was a Newberry Study Bible and his to me a Schofield Reference. David met me at Exeter and brought me back in his car. The front door opened as we approached, and his mother and Aunt Maud welcomed me into their home as if they had known me for years. Mother, years later, volunteered

106

how glad she had been I had called her "Mum" from the start.

I remarked to David how like Mrs. Tilsley (Müller's Director's wife) she looked. Yet another sister, Aunt Daisy, was soon to join us, with her husband Uncle Ed. His broad smile put me completely at ease and very soon the whole family became "mine".

That evening a friend of the family, Aunt Margery, read *Jan Stewer* in Devonshire dialect and we laughed so much we thought our sides would split. David's brother Royston and his wife Grace joined us later for supper making the family complete. It was such a pleasant start to my new Devon experience that it will stay etched in my memory for ever. Family reading and prayers completed that lovely day. Even though I was still working at Chailey Heritage Hospital, and we had to part again all too quickly, it had become obvious that in our love for each other the Lord was supplying a very precious answer to our prayers. We arranged to meet each other as often as possible and it's surprising how love finds a way.

David quickly seemed to sense my need for security and love. My joy was really full when on my birthday, which shortly followed, a beautiful bouquet of spring flowers came to the hospital from my beloved for me. (David of course means 'beloved'). There were red tulips, red, pink and white carnations, daffodils, iris and mimosa, adorned with a sweetly spiritual card. We knew that the Lord had brought us together and earnestly praised Him, as we sought His face for guidance and His will for the future. The nursing staff looked on with great interest.

When David came to Chailey Hospital later that year I kept my promise to introduce him to the children. Many curious eyes followed us wherever we went. All too soon the enjoyable holiday came to an end, but we started to pray about the possibility of a nursing job in Devon for me. The lovely day came when David tenderly asked me to marry him. With great joy we went out to buy a ring. When we arrived at the jewellers David asked me to choose.

I selected one with two diamonds on either side of a ruby stone. I said to my beloved, "It so reminds me of two of Jesus' children bought by His precious blood!" David has always found that a most delightful thought. We will for ever cherish the precious memory of our walk in the park down by the river after our engagement. The birds sang heartily and, framing the river bank, hundreds of golden daffodils waved in the breeze on that sunny morning. We certainly felt the happiest couple in the world.

We had, as I have already mentioned, been praying very much about coming nearer to each other, and on 2nd April 1963 the Lord opened up a nursing post for me in the Maternity Hospital at Heavitree, Devon, as before getting married it seemed necessary to nurse newborn healthy babies. There was such a happy atmosphere at the maternity Hospital between nurses, sisters and other staff. A few of us used to gather for prayer and reading God's word together, and we prayed earnestly for the mothers and their little babies.

One Sunday morning at Heavitice I was on duty and was unable to go and worship at God's house. While I was at work, boiling up a few instruments, I started to hum to myself and then in spontaneous worship started to sing out loud the chorus:

Out there amongst the hills
My Saviour died;
Pierced by those cruel nails,
Was crucified.
Lord Jesus, Thou hast done
All this for me,
Henceforward I would live
Only for Thee.
then:

Rock of Ages cleft for me,
Let me hide myself in Thee,
Let the water and the blood,
From Thy riven side which flowed,

Be of sin the double cure,
Cleanse me from its guilt and power.

A voice called from the side ward. It was one of the mothers who had had her baby, but was in a ward of her own. Joyce was her name.

"Nurse, please come in and see me." I went quickly to her to ask what I could do for her. She burst into tears as she was a bit unsure, having to have a big operation in a week's time. She said, "Please, nurse, I think you can give me the help I am looking for. Please sing those hymns again."

I had been unconscious of anybody hearing me sing praises to my Lord, but Joyce truly was in great need. I asked if I could make sure all the babes and mothers were all right, and told one of the other nurses where I was if I was needed by any of the mothers. Then I went back to the side ward where Joyce was.

"Please sing them again!" So I did. "My," she said, "I have not heard hymns like that sung since I left Sunday school. The first one you sang I do not know. Please sing it again."

"Out there amongst the hills my Savour died," I sang, "pierced by those cruel nails, was crucified. Lord Jesus, Thou hast done all this for me, henceforward I would live only for Thee."

"Tell me more," begged Joyce. I then took out my small Bible from my pocket and opening it I sat by her side to read from *Isaiah 53* "Surely He hath borne our griefs, and carried our sorrows; yet we did esteem Him stricken, smitten of God, and afflicted. But He was wounded for our transgressions, He was bruised for our iniquities: the chastisement of our peace was upon Him; and with His stripes we are healed. All we like sheep have gone astray; we have turned every one to his own way; and the Lord hath laid on Him the iniquity of us all." Then we prayed.

I asked, "Please, loving Heavenly Father, reveal Your lovely Son Jesus Christ to Joyce; she is seeking for You right now. Please may Your powerful Holy Spirit touch her spirit and light her up for the glory of God, in Jesus precious Name. Amen."

I then told her the story of the gypsy boy dying alone at the close of the day. I said "I think I would rather sing the story to you, Joyce".

"Please do," she said. So I sang:-

"Into a tent where the gypsy boy lay,
Dying alone at the close of the day,
News of salvation they carried; said he,
"Nobody ever has told it to me".

Many years ago, I told her, while visiting a camp of gypsies, a Christian missionary found a dying lad in one of the tents. Kneeling by his side, she quoted *John 3v16* slowly three times. "How wonderful!" he said. "I never heard it before. God loves me, a poor gypsy lad. God gave His Son and He said 'whosoever' so that must mean me," said the boy. "I love Him for that." He was then heard to whisper, for he was so ill, "Please tell it to the rest".

"Joyce," I said, "please read with me my dear John 3v16, and put your own name in like this 'For God so loved 'Joyce' that He gave His only begotten Son, that whosoever believeth in Him should not perish but have everlasting life'. God spoke to you, Joyce," I said. "Jesus is asking you to come and thank Him for dying for your sins. You have heard how Jesus loved and died for you in your Sunday school. Please do not keep Him waiting outside your heart's door any longer, for He is calling for you right now."

With this, God's precious word touched her soul and she prayed and asked Jesus to forgive her, and thanked Him for dying for her sins. "When my husband comes in," she said, "I will tell him that Jesus has died for me." She not only did this, but also told her two older children and sent them to Sunday school so they could learn of Jesus and His love for them. She had the operation, got better and was able to go home. We were able to take her husband to hear

110

the wonderful gospel message many times. We pray on for her husband and children.

Here is a hymn David and I often sing together. It was the desire of our heart.

Take my life and let it be,
Consecrated Lord to Thee;
Take my moments and my days,
Let them flow in ceaseless praise.

Take my hands and let them move,
At the impulse of Thy love;
Take my feet and let them be
Swift and beautiful for Thee.

Take my voice and let me sing,
Always, only, for my King;
Take my lips and let them be
Filled with message from Thee.

These were certainly very happy days and precious too, as we prepared for and anticipated our marriage. More and more our prayers centred on the need for a house in which to set up home together.

No suitable property seemed likely to be available in our village where it was necessary for us to live because of David's vocation. Then in March, after a Tuesday night prayer meeting, Mr. and Mrs. Popplestone who lived in the cottage adjoining the Gospel Hall unexpectedly invited us in for supper. During this they explained that they felt the Lord would have them move to Okehampton. Knowing that we intended to get married in September 1964 and were praying about a home, they suggested that we see the head trustee, Mr. Friend, regarding theirs. We bowed our heads and thanked our Lord together, for even on a quick examination we could see great potential.

The cottage was roomy and completely flat downstairs. A few adjustments to the doors we realised would enable even wheelchair bound children to move anywhere freely. This would enable handicapped children to have a lovely holiday spot. Further, the cottage with its adjoining field had originally been purchased by Mr. Henry Soltau on, we undertand, Mr. Müller's behalf. George Muller had then been involved in building the Gospel Hall next door, the property becoming one of his Scripture Knowledge Institutions.

The prospect of moving into such a home was humbling and pleasing. According to the trust though, it had to be advertised widely as it was a missionary training base for many years. Confidently we waited, believing the Lord wanted us to live there and serve Him. Eventually, despite numerous applications, the awaited letter giving us the tenancy arrived, but only just a week before our wedding. We had been much cast upon the Lord and now praised Him from very full hearts.

Our wedding day, September 9th, 1964, was joy-filled indeed. Friends travelled from distant places to the Gospel Hall in Bow, Devon to witness our union and share our joy. The service was conducted by an Evangelist friend, Mr. Goldfinch and with reverent awe we pledged our lives together as we earnestly made our vows. The Evangelist's message was about Aquila and Priscilla in the book of Acts, who used their home and talents to serve the Lord and His people. The message has remained with us for ever. With the prayers of many friends for God's blessing following us, we left for a honeymoon in the Isles of Scilly. It was a precious fortnight. The sunsets over Samson Island viewed from St. Marys stand out vividly in our memories. We so much appreciated the beauty of the flowers, the sunset and the trees while enjoying the presence and love of their Creator as well as of each other.

During the years David and I lived in the Chapel Cottage, we had the joy of remembering great saints of God who had lived there before. Mr. Peter Child, personal friend of Robert Chapman of Barnstaple, came to Bow as an itinerant Evangelist. Finding a teacher's post vacant at Mr. Muller's Day School at the Gospel Hall, he took it, to live in the cottage with his sister for over fifty years. His godliness is remembered with reverence by all who knew him to this day. Mr. and Mrs. Panting trained young missionaries there in subsequent years. Further missionaries, Mr. and Mrs. Harwidge of Malaya and Mr. and Mrs. Ward of India, with their families have occuped the cottage in turn. We ourselves had the joy of living there for sixteen years, worshipping with many other believers in our Lord and Saviour Jesus Christ and sharing in the activities of the Local Assembly.

David studies the Scriptures carefully and teaches God's word over a wide area of Devon. He and I still teach in the Sunday school, David taking over as Superintendent in 1969. David's Uncle Ed had previously been Superintendent for twenty-one years, and his wife Aunt Daisy, David's mum's sister, taught the infant class for sixty years. In 1965 an Evangelist friend of ours, Alwyn Harland, stayed with us to conduct a children's mission in the Village Hall, where for many years Mr. and Mrs. Reg Kimber and their family, taking over a work started by Mr. and Mrs. Jackman, have held a weeknight children's meeting. The mission was a particularly blessed one.

With great joy and wonder we anticipated the birth of our child. We had previously asked guidance of an eminent specialist, Mr. Latimor Short, as to the wisdom of having a family, bearing in mind both our histories of T.B.. I was taken into the City Hospital, Exeter, six weeks before the birth. My nursing friends with whom I had previously nursed were wonderful to me. When our little treasure, God's wonderful gift to us, was finally born we almost instinctively read together the words of *Psalm 103v1* "Bless the Lord, O my soul; and all that is within me, bless His Holy Name".

A mother has no greater joy than to know herself to be the living mother of a living child. Our blessed Lord used it as a fitting type of that wondrous surprise, that strange resurrection joy with which His disciples should find Him, whom they mourned as crucified and dead, to be the living one. *John 16v21 & 22.*

From the 13th August 1965 when our dear daughter Christine Elisabeth was born we have had the great joy of teaching her of Jesus and His love at home and in the Sunday School. How very happy we were when dear Christine embraced the faith for herself, thanking our precious Lord and Saviour Jesus Christ for dying for her as well. She asked if she could follow her Lord in public witness, and was baptized in 1978 on 27th August.

She has for a number of years helped in the Sunday school and Sssembly taking a great share of the organ playing. She played for her friend's wedding when she was only thirteen and a half. Christine followed me into N.N.E.B. training and passed her children's nursing training at eighteen years of age. When Mr. and Mrs. Cowan, present Director of Mullers Homes, came to our present home "Peacehaven Bungalow" for tea, Christine was invited to go to Müller House, Bristol for an interview. She was taken on the staff at Müllers as a children's nurse. During the time Christine has happily worked for Mullers, she has grown to love the children dearly.

When Christine and her friend were asked to sing at the Müller Anniversary in September 1963, Mr. Cowan remarked that to his knowledge this was the first time a daughter of a Müller orphan child had followed her mother into Müllers nursing employment. These Muller Anniversaries have been a great delight and a source of inspiration over 150 years now.

In recent years it has been our special joy to have fellowship with many dear friends, especially a trio of former Muller girls: Miss Edith and Annie Larby and Miss Stewart (Stewie). Their home has ever been open to us and to those who love the Lord. The way our Lord has blessed and guided them through life has been, and still is, an inspiration showing the great faithfulness of our loving Heavenly Father.

My earnest prayer is that my story might help and comfort some dear reader to find a friend in my wonderful Saviour Jesus Christ, who alone can save and cleanse by

His precious blood shed on the cross of Calvary for you. I have written with much prayer, for it has been my true desire to speak forth the praises of my loving Heavenly Father for His great faithfulness and care of me when, out of love, He did not keep me back from deep bodily pain and suffering, this accompanying the loss of my loving parents. the sorrows, pain and trials seemed to come in like mighty billowing waves. In all of it, though, He has shown me that He had a wonderful purpose.

May I say to any dear ones going through such suffering and sorrow, that you feel as if your heart will almost break, "Dry your tears now, dear, weep not all through the night; Jesus is lovingly sympathising for you. Wipe your eyes now in anticipation of the morning. Our tears are dews which mean us as much good as the sunbeams of the morrow."

Yes, your tears clear the eyes for the sight of God in His wonderful grace, and make the vision of His favour more precious. The night of sorrow supplies those shades of the picture by which the highlights are brought out with distinctness. In Hebrews 12v2 we read of our wonderful Jesus who is "the Author and Finisher of our faith, who for the joy set before Him endured the cross, despising the shame."

We can say, "The Lord is our helper; from Him cometh our strength." He has, in His precious Holy Word, a book full of promises and also one for every emergency in life. We believe His promises, for we have personally tried and proved them for ourselves. "For hitherto hath the Lord helped us" *1 Samuel 7v12*.

O child of God, He loveth thee,
And thou art all His own;
With gentle hand He leadeth thee,
Thou dost not walk alone;
And though thou watchest wearily
The long and stormy night,
Yet in the morning joy will come,
and fill thy soul with light.

APPENDIX I

Short History of the Gospel Hall, Bow

In March 1839 Thomas Gribble of Barnstaple, by profession a draper but by now called of God to be a travelling Evangelist, moved from Chittlehamholt via Winkleigh to Bow. During a stay of two years or more, his preaching and devotion was such that many were brought to see a personal responsibility before the living God, and dramatic and lasting changes in lives and homes followed.

Preceding Thomas Gribble's ministry by some years, in the years 1826 – 1830, a simultaneous movement of the Spirit of God, independently and unknown to each other in both Plymouth and Dublin, had resulted in groups of simple Christians renowned for their dedication to the whole truth of the Scriptures, meeting together.

Mr. Gribble himself had, at the time he came to Bow, no formal connections with any movement, simply a desire to preach a challenging Gospel based on God's word. A personal friendship with, and respect for a great saint of God, Robert Chapman of Barnstaple, would certainly have helped to keep this desire true to the Holy Scriptures.

It is almost certainly through Robert Chapman that a man destined to achieve world-wide fame and be an inspiration for God, quoted as "greater than any other in his generation", George Muller of Bristol, became acquainted with these believers at Bow. Though famous for his giant orphanages, Muller's real inspiration was his immense and awe-inspiring faith. Never in possession of money and frequently without the physical food for one breakfast, when he awoke in the morning George Muller cared for two thousand orphans. Some 1,000 more in 70 day schools, and over 28 Sunday Schools in his Scripture Knowledge Institutions. Both in this country and throughout the world he travelled widely, preaching in Europe and Canada and freely distributed thousands of Bibles, and millions of pieces of Gospel literature each year.

His records of unceasing miracles supplying all his needs were meticulously recorded every day for over fifty years, and is one of the wonders of this Christian age.

In the years 1858 – 1860, Muller helped to build the Gospel Hall with the believers in Bow, and it became a Day School plus a Sunday School, but also of course the central meeting place of the believers. Surviving the opening of the state school in 1876 by only a few years, the day school closed, but the Assembly continues to this day. Stories of choice Christians, whose respect and inspiration have reached far beyond the boundaries of Devon, whose home has been spiritual affiliation with the believers in Bow abound. The Hall is still freely used by simple Christians, whose only love is the Lord Jesus Christ and His Glory, and whose chief desire is to glorify Him by unveiling the treasures of His Book.

Mr. and Mrs. Russell Wright at present occupy the Chapel House. Their son-in-law Roger Steer is the author of the most recent books on Mr. George Muller and his work.

APPENDIX II

3 Mullers Orphanage
Ashley Down,
Bristol, 7

24th October 1954

Dear Thelma,

After many years at Ashley Down the time has come for you to leave us. We your friends ask you to accept the Bible, a watch, antler case, water bottle and umbrella as a token of our love for all your cheerful and willing service amongst us.

We realise how hard it must be for you to leave what has been a happy home and a pleasant service after so many years. We shall miss your happy fellowship and kindly, thoughtful ways. We do indeed pray that the nursing you feel called upon to do may be abundantly blessed by our Heavenly Father and we shall remember you very warmly in our prayers.

We all join in sending you our Christian love and pray that God's richest blessing may always be with you.

Mr. and Mrs. McCready, J. J. Rose, J. Cowan, A. Rouse, A. Nute, and ninety-five other signatures.